The Inner Game of Russian Roulette

a Romance of the Soul

by Ananda Mouse

The Inner Game of Russian Roulette

Ananda Mouse

© Betty Ruth Krueger 2008

Published by 1stWorld Publishing
P.O. Box 221, Fairfield, IA 52556
tel: 641-209-5000 • fax: 866-440 5234
web: www.1stworldpublishing.com

First Edition

LCCN: 2008929095
SoftCover ISBN: 978-1-4218-9881-0
HardCover ISBN: 978-1-4218-9880-3
eBook ISBN: 978-1-4218-9882-7

This material has been written and published solely for educational purposes. The author and the publisher shall have neither liability or responsibility to any person or entity with respect to any loss, damage or injury caused or alleged to be caused directly or indirectly by the information contained in this book.

"The writing is exquisite, and the anecdotes are utterly charming; but what makes this book so powerful is the author's ability to bring us along on her journey toward self-realization while sharing some of the most profound concepts about expanding awareness, in such a clear and practical way. Reading this book is like taking Enlightenment 101 with a brilliant professor who also happens to have a grand sense of humor."

—Debra Halperin Poneman, Founder, Yes to Success Seminars, Inc. Amazon Best-Selling Author, *Chicken Soup for the American Idol Soul*

"This charming chronicle of one woman's adventurous quest for enlightenment is at times touching and hilarious. It is a candid and heartfelt inquiry that effortlessly takes you from the ridiculous to the sublime (and back again) in a heartbeat."

—Ceci Balmer, RN, Yoga and Meditation instructor, Editor, *God Loves Fun*, Archive Specialist - Art of Living Foundation

Thank You

To His Holiness Sri Sri Ravi Shankar, for encouraging me
to write and for giving me so much to share.

To Tifrah Warner, for enthusiastic support and many useful suggestions

To Janael McQueen, for patient and thorough attention
to detail, on behalf of the Art of Living Foundation

To Andrew Schulman, for omni-competent assistance
with everything electronic

To Ceci Balmer, Debra Poneman, and Carol Kline for
intelligent critiques and very kind endorsements

To Ed, Leah, and Rodney at 1st World Publishing, for
fabulous teamwork, and for humoring my eccentricities

To all of my indulgent friends, for helpful feedback on
sections of my manuscript at various stages of completion

To my husband, for believing in me and always
being there for me

Table of Contents

Forward

Like every other species on the planet, we humans have an innate urge toward fulfillment. Just as the rosebush is aiming through every cell of every stem, leaf, and thorn to produce an abundance of fully blossomed roses; even so are we, collectively and individually, consciously and unconsciously, aiming with every fiber of our being toward full development of our marvelously immense human potential.

And just as the rosebush in a garden and the rosebush in a wild landscape must draw upon different opportunities of culture and nutrition in the irrepressible quest to "be all I can be;" similarly, we humans draw upon different opportunities for growth in our varied surroundings. Some of us find guidance and inspiration through religious worship and the study of scriptures. Some of us pursue self-development through disciplines such as meditation, yoga, or self-inquiry. Some of us grow and bloom by simply following in the footsteps of our elders as we, in turn, negotiate the challenges of youth, adulthood, and old age.

But there is one particular in which we differ from the rosebush—as well as, to a great extent, from every other life-form on our planet—and that is, *we humans require to learn from other humans how to be human.*

To realize its innate aim to flower in abundance, the rose-bush experiences no need for guidance or inspiration from sacred rosebush lore handed down from olden times. It doesn't learn and practice disciplines for rosebush self-development. It doesn't rely upon elder rosebushes as role models to show it how to produce stems, leaves, thorns, and petals at the appropriate times and places. The rosebush can take full advantage of the sunshine, the rain, and the nutrients in the soil to fulfill its ultimate purpose in life, even if there are not now, and never have been, any other rosebushes anywhere in its vicinity.

Not so the human being. We are a *culture generating* and *culture-dependent* species. In the natural scheme of things, it is entirely up to us to provide the nurturing context we require in order to manifest our own inherent potential. Even to pursue such survival basics as what, when, where and how to eat, we rely upon a substantial fund of accu-mulated and preserved knowledge from our collective past. Communication with fellow humanity is critical to every aspect of our lives; and communication requires language —which we learn almost entirely by hearing and imitating other people. Even though the potential for language is provided by nature in the structure of our brains, if we happen to be raised from infancy by a pack of wolves, we will learn to communicate through barks, growls, howls, and grunts—and not until we begin to interact with fellow humans will we learn to use human language.

Arguably, the most time-honored and influential context

for human growth and development would be the mentor relationship. We all rely upon it in infancy and childhood, as we imbibe most of the survival basics, along with a great many fundamental norms and customs, from our parents and primary care-givers. Throughout much of human history, vocational skills of every kind have been either passed down from parents and other relatives to their children, or acquired through tutoring and apprenticeship. Even though formal education today relies more heavily upon books, computers, and relatively impersonal classroom settings, we almost instinctively reach out for the more personal assistance of mentors and counselors at critical junctures of personal, professional, and spiritual life.

Despite its central importance to the human story, the mentoring relationship receives far less attention in the annals of Western literature than the nearly omnipresent drama of the mating relationship. And yet, in the experience of this writer, the compelling depth, power, and inspiration that can be evoked in a mentoring relationship at least rivals the profundity we commonly associate with themes of romantic love.

My first impulse to help redress this imbalance dates to a suggestion in the summer of 1993, from my personal and spiritual mentor, to "write about your experiences." The volume you have in your hands is excerpted from the odyssey of verbal self-expression that he continues to encourage me to indulge. The pen-name persona I refer to as "Ananda Mouse" is a doodle from the margins of my original manuscript, who gradually evolves into one of its unifying metaphors. I invite you to enjoy my literary collaboration with her playful skirmishes.

Betty Ruth Krueger

January, 2008

for
Esther Mae
my heart's first mentor

About the author

The eldest of six in a family who rarely miss a service at their rural Midwestern Protestant church, Ananda, like her ancestors, grows up on a diet of King James Bibles, hymnals, prayer books, and catechisms. As one of the first among her kin to venture onto a liberal arts campus, she spends her restless young adulthood gnawing through tomes of a more free-thinking nature, and develops a particular fondness for the word "liberation," along with all of its synonyms. Readers may chance to see her scampering about the feet of various enlightened masters. Generally she prefers the Eastern ones for their practice of *ahimsa* (non-violence to all creatures).

Her favorite living saint is Sri Sri Ravi Shankar, of the venerated Shankaracharya lineage, whose voluminous and

light-hearted commentaries upon liberated maturity draw
wisdom and inspiration from several of the world's major
spiritual traditions.

Invoking the blessings of the Elephant-headed *Ganesh*,
Remover of Obstacles (and Divine Protector of Mice),
Ananda wishes you good fortune through the reading of
her journal.

Om Shri Ganeshaya
Namaha

Prequel to Chapter One

LIBERATION AS A HAUNTED HOUSE

Hi! I'm Ananda. Ananda Mouse. It's a pen name, of course. In Reality, I am you and you are me (and we are one—you probably know the words to the song). Or, in other words, I am Nobody, or maybe Everybody, depending on your point of view. But that is getting way ahead of my story.

For the time being (circa 1969), and circumstantially speaking, I am a student at a small Mid-western university. In terms of passion and personal identity, I am a feminist. I am determined to make my voice heard and my life count toward seeing the rights and freedoms of democracy fully extended to members of my own sex. The theme of my young life is pretty well summed up in the four words of my favorite slogan: "Liberation Begins with Me."

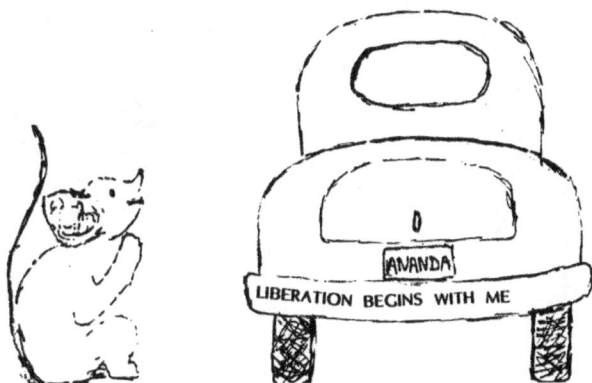

ANANDA

LIBERATION BEGINS WITH ME

Through practical efforts to bring more democratic fairness into the details of everyday life, I become aware that some of my ingrained cultural habits, traditions, and attitudes need to be questioned and revised. This requires self-examination (a process referred to as "consciousness raising" in feminist circles). It also brings home to me that the chief ongoing purpose of culture is precisely what the term implies: to *cultivate* and *nurture* the blossoming of human potential. To better understand the influences that shape my own unfolding, I embark upon a journey into humanistic psychology, aiming for a career in psychotherapy. My fascination with culture leads me to explore approaches to self-development that are related to, inspired by, or derived from other eras, cultures, and traditions.

Ananda Mouse

Having ideals is one thing. Living up to them is something else. Pursuing the carrot of liberation proves to be somewhat like exploring the ultimate haunted house. It is as if I wander into a stately edifice and stumble upon hidden chambers which open into secret passageways that land me on the other side of the world at the other end of time. Liberation, in the democratic sense, is about as modern and Western a notion as I could ask for. But its ramifications lure me into non-Western perspectives deriving from remnants of legend, myth, and oral tradition that reach beyond the range of recorded history.

It is an expedition that certainly has its spooky moments.

I am not the only member of my college circle who feels a pull in non-Western directions. I have a girlfriend who belongs to a group of Krishna devotees. Most of us feel that there is something special about her. She is warm, gregarious, and fun-loving; and there is a certain quiet evenness that one feels around her. She can calmly deal with hassles that throw me into hysteria. Her boyfriends last rarely longer than a few months at a stretch, a pattern similar to my own. But her ex-lovers seem to revere her as a kind of feminine prototype, and hardly hold it against her when she moves on to another. My own relationship transitions seem far less graceful.

I wonder if there is something in my friend's exotic devotional life which might account for her exceptional qualities. I have almost decided to ask her to introduce me to her spiritual path, when one day she gets a letter from its headquarters. The letter informs her that she is to be married to a fellow devotee, whom she has never met, in another city. To my utter astonishment, my friend obeys the summons, leaving her studies, friends, and current lover to participate in a group marriage at the behest of her spiritual master.

In subsequent months, she writes letters referring to herself and her new spouse by Indian names, and describing him as "one fine devotee." She details life in a spiritual center where communal values are observed which exceed communist ideals, and where even married men and women live in separate quarters. Within a year she has a baby, and we are introduced to ideas of educating children which emphasize mainly the worship of Krishna.

These glimpses of my friend's spiritual lifestyle suggest an overall picture so divergent from Western values that it totally "blows my mind." Every time I see the Krishna devotees with their robes and shaved heads selling books at the airports, I think about my friend. I remember the devotional quality of her life, which subtly charms me. And I wonder about her unquestioning submission to authority, which genuinely alarms me.

Haunted houses have a way of being charming and eerie, both at once.

I continue to feel attracted to non-Western notions of liberation, but an element of caution comes into my steps. I feel wary of the possibility that I might get drawn into something seriously at odds with my cherished Western-value claims to personal liberty. I want to pursue the inward, Eastern values of liberation, without sacrificing the outward, Western variety.

Eventually, a Transcendental Meditation instructor shows up on our campus. He speaks about something called a mantra, which sounds pretty far out. But most of his lecture emphasizes stress release, personal growth, and world peace. He isn't wearing robes, and doesn't shave his head. But he does shave his beard, and his hair is short, even though he is about my own age. Also, he is wearing a suit and tie; and his demeanor reminds me of a little kid putting on his best Sunday School behavior. In an era of long hair, beards, fringes, beads, blue-jean bells, and rebellious attitudes, this guy looks almost as embarrassingly odd as the airport devotees. I feel somewhat suspicious of his claim that you can practice "TM" (as he calls it) without any change in personal beliefs or lifestyle.

Still, the benefits he is describing sound similar to the qualities I admire in my devotee girlfriend. Plus, making a contribution to world peace is another of my ardent objectives in life. If that really is what *Maharishi* ("great seer," the title of TM's founder) has in mind, maybe he won't object if his Western practitioners keep to their freedom-loving lifestyles. I have a close friend who is already meditating, and she assures me that it really is a self-sufficient practice. Her boyfriend and I are the only two who show up for the next initiation.

The experience evokes an unexpectedly deep response in me. I am quickly convinced that my instructor's claims are not exaggerated. Meditation definitely leaves me calmer and more centered. It clearly helps me handle stress better. It does seem to open up internal resources of creativity and energy. The potential contribution to world peace seems entirely credible. Within weeks I am rearranging my whole life on the basis of it. Instead of my goal to become a psychotherapist, I decide to be a meditation instructor. I feel I can do more good by introducing people to meditative transcendence, than by merely counseling them about their problems.

Many of my friends and family now view me in a way that is similar to how I regard my Krishna-worshipping friend. On the one hand, they appreciate and applaud the positive changes they observe in me. But on the other hand, isn't there something a little odd about the abrupt new direction I am taking with my life?

From my side, the mysterious behavior of my devotee girlfriend seems a little more understandable. I see for myself how there can be something so compelling about an experience, that it becomes almost impossible not to orient significantly toward it. I feel like my new decisions are the most natural and obvious in the world for me to make, even though they look almost as bizarre to some people as my friend's unusual marriage looks to me.

Internally, I sense that I may be crossing over some kind of boundary beyond which one does not return—as if somewhere behind me a heavy door is quietly sliding shut. Mentally, I reassess my position: Ok, so some of my friends and most of my large, close-knit family are definitely "wierded-out" by my unimaginable career decision. But on the other hand, some of my best friends are delving into the meditative experience with me, and my circle of meditating acquaintances is rapidly widening. Also, my favorite psychology professor has some very positive and intriguing things to say about the expanded possibilities available to human experience through yogic practices of meditation.

But most importantly, the prospect of forging ahead in this new, unfamiliar direction appears challenging and exciting to me, whereas the idea of retracing my steps—of returning to my former plans and goals—takes on a dull and boring hue. Actually, it goes even deeper than that. Some kind of primordial instinct has been aroused in my soul, hearkening to the call of this adventure. It is as if I have uncovered a smoldering ember buried in the fire pit of some long-forgotten hearth, devoutly refusing to be extinguished.

OK, so wherever it may lead, and regardless of what friends and family may think, this is a journey I have to make. But I'm not going to let it charm me into relinquishing the values and beliefs which already form the basis of my personal sense of integrity. About this, also, I am firmly resolved.

If anything, TM's fascinating founder, Maharishi Mahesh Yogi, seems to go out of his way to reassure individuals like myself. His basic instruction is to spend twenty minutes morning and evening meditating, and otherwise go on about living your life. As I move into the training program for becoming an instructor, I am gratified to learn that he does not expect even his teachers to view themselves as disciples or devotees, but rather as fellow dedicates to the higher cause of bringing peace to our troubled planet. I feel no reservation about anything he says.

During the Teacher Training Course, we are exposed to in-depth discussions of Maharishi's deeply surrendered attunement to his personal spiritual master. He clearly wants us to understand and appreciate his wish that all credit for his accomplishments be laid at the feet of his late beloved Guru Dev. His tender stories of his years in his master's ashram present an intriguing new perspective for me, of the beauty and intimacy and expanded personal growth that are possible through human relationship. But I also view this type of relationship as appropriate to another cultural context than my own, and feel grateful to Maharishi for having the insight and the competence to isolate a group of effective techniques for liberation, and adapt them to the more self-sufficient Western lifestyle.

I feel vindicated in my viewpoint when our course leaders explain to us that Maharishi is a special individual with a particular *dharma* (life-work) to fulfill—i. e., world peace —and that the appropriate way to attune oneself to him is to attune oneself to his work. In this connection, we are admonished that it is inappropriate to ask him personal questions. Some of my fellow teacher-trainees grumble over this restriction, but for me it is perfect. Even though I revere this exceptional man more highly than anyone else I have met, the last thing in the world I want is any kind of outside authority imposed upon my personal life. I defi-nitely prefer to make my own decisions by applying such wisdom as may come my way, according to my own increasingly brightening lights.

According to Maharishi's teachings, there comes a point where actual personal interaction with an enlightened pre-ceptor becomes necessary for further liberation, but not until one has progressed beyond the fifth and sixth "states of consciousness." In any case, we are assured that "when the student is ready, the master appears." I decide to pass through those exalted portals when I come to them.

For well over a decade, nothing seems to seriously chal-lenge my assumption that liberation is a goal that can be pursued and progressively attained upon my own terms. I marry a fellow meditation instructor, and the two of us dedicate ourselves to making the knowledge and techniques of meditation available in the various cities where we live. In practical terms, what that mostly means is that my husband financially supports my philanthropic endeavors. But even though our meditation centers never become financially self-supporting, they do afford us many rewarding experiences, along with a comforting sense that at least we are making a positive contribution to the world in which we live.

My family and non-meditating friends gradually adjust to the fact that I really am determined to pursue this unusual career. A few of them actually learn TM and become genuinely appreciative of its value. Some of my relatives still prefer to change the subject whenever meditation happens to come up in conversation, but all of them really like my husband and warmly receive us at family gatherings and celebrations. All in all, it seems as though that ardently smoldering ember in the fire-pit of my haunted hearth has been kindled into a safe and cheerful domestic fire.

But somewhere in the universe there is a rule that haunted houses may not be domesticated. Perhaps they represent territory that has been reclaimed by the wilder spirits of nature, who sometimes feel a need to dispel our illusions about who is in control.

About fifteen years into my career, my husband and I learn that we are to become parents. Our delight is shadowed, however, by some serious health problems that my forty-year-old body manifests in response to this demand. My doctor orders me to stop working and observe absolute bed rest. Our meditation center has to be closed, since there are no other instructors in our area to take over the responsibility. After a few months, I lose our baby, and spend six weeks in the hospital fighting for my own life. Heroic medicine saves me; but the necessary surgeries traumatize my system, and my meditation experiences are drastically compromised.

When I am strong enough to travel, I return to the home we have purchased in the small Mid-western town where the TM organization's largest US establishment is located. I apply to our select team of traditional Ayurvedic practitioners, chosen by Maharishi himself, for solutions to my new and unfamiliar health concerns. I face the task of adjusting my accomplishment-oriented personality to the limitations of an extended convalescence, which isn't easy for me. I expect my repertoire of TM practices to blissfully come to my aid, but meditation in my current condition isn't taking me to the levels of rest and rejuvenation to which I am accustomed. The TM organization's medical advisors won't allow me to enroll in any of their advanced programs until my surgical wounds are healed. Rest and Ayurveda become my prescribed agenda.

In many ways the Ayurvedic programs are wonderfully helpful, but certain troublesome issues persist. Our finances are strained. The Ayurvedic treatments are of course not free, and mostly not covered by insurance. My frustration level is mounting. It isn't just the money. Part of the problem is that there is a conspicuous *sexual* dimension to my unresolved health issues. The abdominal surgery seems to have trapped a lot of energy in the lower half of my body. The advanced meditation techniques I have been practicing for years depend upon an intact neurological substrate, and mine is seriously compromised. But TM's organizational representatives, including the health practitioners, almost unilaterally shun the subject of sex.

I seek counsel with myself. My spiritual reality is changing into something almost unrecognizable. The familiar terrain of transcendence and serenity is giving way to a wilderness of lust and loss and frustration. It is as if my cheerful domestic hearth fire has become a raging house fire, driving me into subterranean passageways of quest and self-inquiry, from where I can only watch as my peacefully simmering evolutionary lifestyle drifts away like smoke among the clouds.

In despair, I think of Maharishi, the gentle, compassionate visionary who wants so much for our world. How can I "attune myself to his work" in the condition I am in? Where is the wisdom for me in all this?

I have a friend who is trying to introduce me to a new chiropractic program that is available in a nearby larger city. Suddenly, her appeal sounds interesting. I look into my health insurance plan, and learn that the same policy that is shelling out twenty grand for the expenses related to my recent hospital stay, also offers generous coverage for chiropractic care. What do I have to lose?

Soon my friend and I are traveling twice a week to this long-haired Greek chiropractor whose energy and vitality alone are almost enough to banish subluxation. His unusual system of care immediately begins to restore some measure of credibility to my wimpy meditation experiences. He notices the discomfort I am feeling with the intensified sexuality in my body, and schedules a Neuro-Linguistic Programming session to help me orient to it more constructively. He recommends a body-worker to help me better integrate his treatments. In return for driving her to the chiropractor, my friend gives me sessions in Educational Kinesiology, a healing modality she is accredited to practice.

Even though this combination of care falls into my life almost haphazardly, it delivers progress toward recovery in the troublesome areas that seem to defy the more meticulously controlled Ayurvedic approach. I suspect that I may have some lessons to learn along the lines of "letting go and letting God," as the saying goes.

In fact, "lessons to learn" are bombarding me thick and fast from every direction. My chiropractor and my body-worker both emphasize that I am sabotaging my own healing by counterproductive habits of thought. I need to get "out of my head" and "in my body." It is also apparent that I have a lot of unresolved grief to deal with from the loss of my miscarried child. As I delve deeply into physical and emotional release, some ancient memories come up, obviously from previous lives—or, to put it more precisely, previous *deaths*. In my case, such recollections are not at all glamorous. Although they convey pertinent truths, I find it challenging to try to assimilate them.

My body-worker, who is quite intuitive, offers the insight that I need to nurture through touch, as I would be doing if I had been able to bring my child into the world. He suggests that I learn some type of massage therapy. The idea appeals to me, and I enroll in the training needed for certification in a form of educational bodywork.

So now my health is improving and I am embarking upon a new career. These are blessings, and I am grateful for them; but there is a restlessness in my soul, along with a nagging sense of uncertainty about where I am going with my life. Everything seems to be just kind of happening *to* me, as if I have lost my moorings and become entirely subject to the caprice of unpredictable currents and tides. I yearn for some resource of broadly competent personal guidance.

The elderly Maharishi no longer travels, and few are

privileged to go and see him. One day it is announced in our meditation hall that his chief spokesperson is in town and scheduled to give a talk. Such events are always well-attended, featuring the latest news from Maharishi, along with anecdotal accounts of some of his activities. I arrive, in the company of several hundred fellow meditators, at the appointed time.

As I step out of my shoes and enter the peaceful interior of the clear-span geodesic dome where gatherings of our meditating community take place, I am aware of a faint intonation of sadness in my soul. I settle into the familiar comfort of a pillow-covered back support on the foam-cushioned floor, and close my eyes to listen to the orchestra within.

As if from a distance, I overhear the usual flourishes of exaggerated praise being offered to the speaker by way of introduction, followed by his usual responses of embarrassed humility. I open my eyes and look at him, noticing that he possesses the type of strong but corpulent physique that can often be observed in Western men who wield power. There is sincerity and dedication in his voice as he warms up to his inspirational and somewhat rhetorical style. But my heart is not responding. My undertone of sadness surfaces in the recognition that I no longer innocently and open-heartedly feel like I am an integral part of all that is happening here. I tell myself that there is no reason to jump to such a conclusion, but the feeling doesn't change. I sense that my heart is resonating with some kind of deeper intuition than is available to my mind.

I absently follow the sound of the speaker's voice as he talks about Maharishi sending him on a tour to visit certain notable Indian saints. Coming into the presence of a saint is reputed to confer spiritual grace. Perhaps that is what I need. A resolution takes form in my mind: *I am going to go and see some saints.*

I don't know how, exactly. I certainly do not have the funds for a trip to India. But I soon learn that there are in fact a number of liberated individuals who regularly cir-cumambulate the globe, similarly as our own Maharishi used to do. Some of their tours even include major Mid-western cities...

Ananda Mouse

Darshan is a Sanskrit term, usually translated to mean *vision*, or *presence*. The "darshan of a saint" might be described as a kind of immersion in presence. There is a deeply interactive element of seeing and being seen, knowing and being known—but words are inadequate to capture the experience, which is quite unlike anything else in the world.

Indeed, perhaps it isn't really *in* the world. Coming into the presence of a saint can be like wandering into the proverbial enchanted oasis. There may be dozens, hundreds, even thousands of people in the vicinity, milling about, talking, chanting, the buying and selling of books, pictures, sacred jewelry, etc.—and yet the tranquility in the space remains almost tangibly undisturbed. Questions, concerns, and urgencies of every kind can melt away in an instant, in the presence of a realized being. Different people experience such things to varying degrees of intensity. In my case, it is generally quite compelling. Waves of peace steal over my soul, transporting me into a timelessness in which absolutely nothing matters, and yet everything is utterly precious.

Visiting saints is definitely helping me handle the turbulence of my life. Sometimes they offer words of wisdom and guidance, or teach helpful practices. Sometimes they just surround everyone with nurturing love and acceptance. None of them offers to solve my problems for me. But coming into their presence pulls me back deeply into my own center, endowing my soul with renewed enthusiasm for the challenge of steering my own course wisely.

In my pilgrimages to the enlightened, I honestly don't know whether I am looking for a long-term personal connection, or am just here for the nourishment of the moment. And even if I do want a personal relationship, I have no idea how such a thing might be brought about. But in the presence of one who has "crossed over the sea of bondage," even this question dissolves into meaninglessness. Somehow I know just to participate in whatever structure, or non-structure, is provided; and the perfect thing will happen, or not, at the perfect when or never.

Thus my life is blessed by the grace of several radiant beings who truly live somewhere beyond our ordinary range of time and relativity. Most of these venerable souls hail from remote areas of the world where ancient ways are kept alive, and literally embody values and traditions that hearken back to pre-historic eras of the human saga. In a very real sense, my haunted halls and passages of quest and inquiry are drawing me into the celestial daylight of enchanted places in immemorial time.

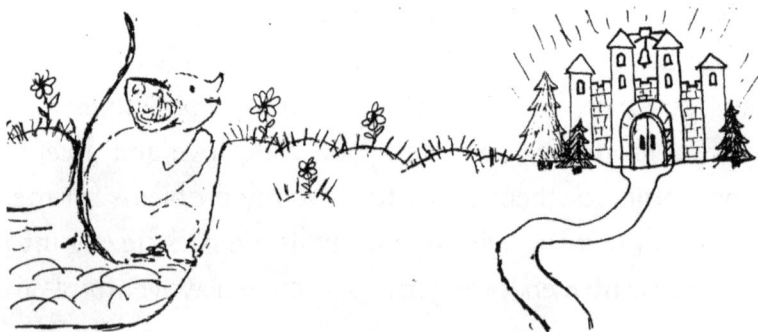

Ananda Mouse

Chapter One

THE YIN-YANG OF
SURRENDER AND LOVE

The Question Basket is one of the classic features of a meditation retreat with the Indian spiritual master Sri Sri Ravi Shankar, affectionately addressed by his followers as simply "Sri Sri," "Guruji," or "Gurudev."

Actually, there will be two baskets: one for "Questions," and the other for "Botherations." Notes deposited in the Question Basket are selectively read and answered, or not answered, by Sri Sri in daily group meetings. Notes left in the Botherations Basket are generally not read aloud, but presumably attended to according to their merits.

The practical purpose of the baskets is to enable communication to take place while retreat participants are observing a regimen of meditative silence. For me, however, this simple system cloaks a seductive dynamic, which I privately refer to as the "inner game of Russian roulette." As soon as the two innocent-looking baskets get introduced into our course routine, it is as though I become compulsively driven to spend my days of silence triggering the cocked pistol of the master's unpredictable wit and wisdom against the temples of my personal ego.

I scamper into this cleverly devised little mind trap quite unsuspectingly during my very first encounter with Sri Sri. I am at a point in my life where I consider myself to be an experienced and fairly competent spiritual seeker. I have taught and faithfully practiced techniques of meditation and yoga for nearly twenty years. I have received personal darshan from a number of revered living saints. I am developing my skills as an alternative health practitioner. I am well versed in the cutting-edge literature of the New Age. In general, it seems to me that I am applying enlightened principles to my daily life with a respectable degree of success.

Although I have been familiar with Sri Sri's practice of *Sudarshan Kriya* for only a few weeks, I feel that I know exactly what its contribution is going to be to my personal evolution. And I am also pretty sure about just what sort of spiritual guidance I wish to solicit from the master himself. In my first contribution to the Question Basket, I waste no time in coming right to the point:

"Dear Sri Sri,

"During the past two years, I have been drawn to various types of techniques related to *prana* [life energy] and the breath. As I tried various programs that came my way, I became aware that this is a very powerful realm of spiritual life; and I began to desire the guidance of a master in this area. You are the obvious answer to that desire, and I would like your advice on pursuing this area in general:

"May I safely follow my own intuition and experience in regard to other prana-oriented techniques I am familiar with—particularly Tai Chi and Chi Kung exercises—but did not learn from realized masters? What about learning such practices from books that have been written by actual masters in their areas? I think this question may interest many other members of this course, especially if in the 'books' part you include the various works on Tantric and Taoist sex practices which many spiritually minded people turn to, to avoid depletion of energy in married life. Thank you."

Sri Sri, in return, wastes no time in coming right to the point with me.

"You may have in your drawer two dozen spoons," he replies. "But when you have to drink the soup, you can't have four spoons and drink the soup."

Laughter ripples across the room.

"If you put four spoons in the soup and take it, soup will be in none of them."

The absurdity of the image provokes even more laughter. (I have already noticed that Sri Sri likes to capitalize upon humor.)

"One spoon is enough to drink the soup."

The ripples of laughter gradually subside as Sri Sri continues, his melodious voice selecting softer tones from a slightly lower register:

"I have nothing against you learning more techniques and knowledge. But know that to just go on collecting techniques... It's not like a stamp collection. It's no use. You can only satisfy your ego.—'I have learned so many techniques. I know it all.'

"Drop all this and sit, in surrender, in love. You will see you will blossom." By the end of his answer, Sri Sri is speaking quietly, barely above a whisper. A contemplative hush pervades the room.

Sitting amidst the shattered smithereens of my spiritually responsible, take-the-bull-by-the-horns persona, all I can hear is the echo of laughter in the cavern of my mind, and the quiet resonance of tenderness and compassion in Sri Sri's voice. I feel exposed and vulnerable, and at the same time, deeply honored. His simple answer has abruptly shifted my perspective, speaking volumes to me in a new language.

I am startled to perceive that there is something slightly irreverent, even flippant, in my personal approach to God. It appears that I have allowed myself to become foolishly impressed by my own busy achieverishness. In fact, my entire personality suddenly seems like a silly masquerade. I really can't blame Sri Sri for not even wanting to relate to it.

But he obviously does want to relate to me, and without any kind of farcical trappings in the way. *"Drop all this and sit, in surrender, in love."* Re-echoing in my mind's ear, his words hold me spellbound. I perceive that I am being invited to relate in terms of the utmost intimacy to the master or to God, I'm not quite sure which.

I am also not quite sure *how*. Although my life is rich to the point of turbulence with currents of intense and passionate love, *surrender* could not be said to be a prominent feature of my behavioral repertoire. Love certainly is one of my higher values, which I often find myself devotedly or eagerly pursuing, in its various forms. But love as something to be quietly and intimately surrendered into? Well, it's a beautiful idea, just not what typically happens with me. Most of my experience of life leads me to believe that I will probably be pretty good at anything I attempt to do, but I feel some misgiving that *surrender* is going to be one of those exceptional cases of something I might not have very much natural talent for.

I'm not feeling quite ready to submit my uncertainties about surrender to the Question Basket, but someone else's question on the subject is soon read out:

"Dear Gurudev,

"Could you say more about surrender? Does one surrender to one's enemy so that they have no power over one? ...I thought surrender is giving oneself to the other. Thank you."

"Surrender," he replies, "is one of the unfortunate words which has been misunderstood, many times. We think surrender means when a person loses. Say suppose a person loses a war, they surrender. But you know, they have not really surrendered. They are just waiting for an opportunity to jump back. This is one type of surrender, or so-called surrender. Submission.

"Surrender here is being in total love, total trust and love. Like, say suppose, a mother. A mother has planned to go to a party. But the child gets sick. The mother doesn't say, 'Oh, I have surrendered going to the party because of my child.' No ...It is just the love that draws her heart. 'OK, I have to attend to my child now.' She doesn't feel a pinch of not going to the party.

"Surrender is dropping all that fear, tension, frustration, negativity, everything,—just dumping them. Feeling free —hollow and empty. It is your very nature. You are born with the quality that is called surrender."

I feel somewhat reassured. But I also feel that I probably wouldn't measure up to Gurudev's standards of motherhood, were I ever to become one.

On the other hand, I do have a sense of what he is talking

about. It brings up my recent experience of pregnancy, of relaxing into the physical and emotional flow of nature's life-creating miracle. But then I lose my baby after only a few months through a traumatic miscarriage, and spend six weeks in the hospital fighting for my own life. I am still recovering from this, emotionally and physically.

My mind wanders to the words of another saint, who advises me to love God as my child—to see the Divine in everyone, and to love that Divine as my own dearly beloved child. I am observing his advice as best I can, and find it healing to my heart. There is also a lady saint who rekindles my own experience of infancy by taking me into her arms and pressing my head softly into her chest, while chanting *Ma Ma Ma Ma*. She speaks very little English, but takes people of all ages into her lap and hugs them during darshan. I revere her deeply, and feel I have a lot to learn from her about motherhood, Divine and human...

The discussion comes to an end, and Sri Sri instructs us to settle in for the afternoon meditations. He leads us through a sequence of guided sessions in which a deeply meditative consciousness gently flows through various parts of the body. Listening from my transcendent perspective to the sound of Sri Sri's voice, I begin to experience him—his wisdom, his tenderness, his love—as being inside of me, in exactly the same way as I experienced the child inside my womb. My heart is flowing to him as simply and unreservedly as she was flowing to my precious unborn child. I hold my tears somewhat in check, so as not to disturb the group.

The same experience recurs during my private meditations in the evening, and again when I wake up during the night. Being alone, I let my tears flow freely. I know that in part I am completing the grieving process that began when I lost my child. But I seem to be feeling a lot more than grief. There is a sense of melting, dissolving, cleansing, merging. Could this be what Gurudev means by surrender?

Maybe, but that word still makes me nervous.

In the morning, I awake feeling like a child myself. Everything looks dewy and fresh and kind of sparkly, as in early spring—even though this is a dry California winter day. I feel delicate and hopeful and vulnerable, like a tender new leaf opening up to the sunshine. I am grateful for the privacy afforded by our silence. I sense that I am going through some kind of internal reorganization as a result of yesterday's shift in perspective. More questions are coming up in my mind.

The deepest shift seems to involve my feelings and attitudes toward saints and Divine personalities. I sense that my reverence for the Divine in all its forms is becoming more a concern of my heart and less a concern of my mind. I decide to inquire via the Question Basket upon how to properly conduct emotional relationships with Divine and realized beings. I contribute a longish note, which Sri Sri edits down into two separate sections:

"Dear Guruji,

"You say realized souls can still feel negative emotions. Does that include jealousy and/or betrayal? Could it happen that a realized master could get upset seeing his or her devotees at the feet of another master? Is there such a thing as spiritual infidelity?"

With the simplicity of a child, Guruji first inquires about the meaning of the word "infidelity." Apparently, he is still teaching himself English. Then he proceeds to deliver his answer with all the natural authority of the most venerable sage:

"This is not possible," he declares. "At the most, a realized person would feel compassion in such cases where people are going astray. At the most, compassion.

"What is jealousy? Jealousy is not knowing who you are. Jealousy is not knowing how unique you are, how wonderful you are, how great you are. And jealousy is not knowing the time and life span.

"Jealousy is not feeling one with everyone around you, isn't it? Whomsoever you feel jealous about, you make them part of you. You will see, will you feel jealous about them? Not possible! Jealousy comes, or any of these negative emotions come, when they are not part of you, when they are different from you, when you see them different, when there is the competitive spirit of 'I also want to be like that.' You are already like that!

"You can't be everything. Can you be everything? Can you

be a scientist? 'I want to be independent, self-sufficient.' This self-sufficient word is also very much mistaken. What is self-sufficiency? Don't you depend on a doctor? Don't you depend on a lawyer? Don't you depend on the city corporation for supply of electricity, water, etc.? Don't you depend on the farmer to give you food? Don't you depend on the education system to teach you ABCDXYZ? 'Bah Bah Black Sheep, Have You Any Wool?'"

We all burst into laughter, delighted by his genius for comic relief. As soon as we can hear him again, he continues, "You have not made the 'Bah Bah Black Sheep.' Somebody made that. Even that song, that melody, you borrowed it from somebody. 'Bah Bah Black Sheep, Have You Any Wool?' A simple person somewhere in some corner of the village made this song; and today it is all over the world what millions of children learn. 'Twinkle Twinkle Little Star.' You see?

"What is self-sufficiency? This is a real illusion in our mind. 'I am somebody. I am somebody. I am different.' This causes even more tension.

"'Everybody is mine,' OK. 'In all these different forms and shapes and talents, it's all me only. I have wonderful talent in that body as a cook. I have wonderful talent in that body as a tailor, and wonderful talent in that body as a doctor.' Making yourself not different from everyone. Bringing them all together, like a flower bunch, like a bouquet. This is the way to get over your negative feelings. It is just ignorance, that's all."

Guruji is not letting me off the hook, I can see that. If I want him to consider a question about jealousy among saints, I also have to be willing to consider what is in my own heart. Jealousy is in fact a problem in my life, beginning from early childhood, when I become entangled in a painful sibling rivalry that springs up between myself and the sister next to me in age.

I invoke the memory of my sister cruelly taunting me at the dinner table when it is my turn to perform the hated task of washing the dishes. As usual, my parents are indulgently letting her get away with this. I very well know that were I to behave as hatefully toward her, I would be punished. But she basks in the sunshine of their love, while I mostly draw the thunderclouds of parental disapproval. Their blatant partiality to her makes me want to scream and throw tantrums, which sometimes I do. But my parents never get the point. Eventually I give up on them and turn to teachers and friends for emotional support.

In adulthood I maintain a cordial orientation toward my family, but my heart still harbors the pain of an as yet unresolved emotional estrangement. I try to imagine my sister as part of myself in the dinner-table scenario. Childish emotions of hurt and rebellion flood my heart. This is not going to be easy.

Meanwhile, the second part of my question is being read:

"My childhood was dominated by love of Christ; and later when I read the *Mahabharata* and *Ramayana* [ancient epic scriptures of India], I fell in love with Krishna and Rama. To me they are the same thing, as are Shiva and the Holy Spirit, Mother Mary and Mother Divine, etc. But do they feel that way? Why do the scriptures of both traditions speak of jealous divinities? Is it just a misinterpretation?"

"Now," begins Guruji, in a tone of voice that signals the reader to put down her microphone, and suggests to the rest of us to settle in for something that is going to go a little deeper. "We considered all these emotions as part of the game, as play, so that you could be at ease. If you think it is a war, you'll not be at ease. But a game—the winning or losing in a game does not have much significance, does it? And this is true. An emotion comes, something kindled in your system…

"I tell you, love is the greatest power. Here, one who surrenders, wins. Love is the greatest power on earth. Surrender is the greatest power. When you are surrendered, you become so powerful, even more powerful than any angel. When you live that state of love, all the angels and gods, all the beings, come to serve you. You have nothing to do, nothing to get. No need to take knowledge or wisdom from anybody, even the angels. Nor wealth from the Goddess of Wealth.

"You have come alone on this planet, haven't you? And you will go alone. Just remember this: You have come alone, and you will go alone. What do you need here? What is it you want here, thirty-forty years when you are here? Can you be just happy?

"You have come here to give something, contribute some-thing. Whatever you could do to people, do it, from your side. Finished. Very simple.

"There is a beautiful couplet in *Tamil*, one of the Indian languages. Says, 'If at all you have to ask anything, pray for anything, pray for love, so that your heart can blossom, be in love all the time.' If there is anything worth asking for, ask for love.

"Because even that is a gift. It is not something that you could be proud of, that you have cultivated inside you or cultured inside you. That is a gift. That's what is given in between the words. It's not given in words, it comes between the gap of the words. Words are like the thermo-col. You know? Thermocol—packing material? In between them there is a gap, where they put anything,—micro-phone, whatever."

It is a strange and provocative answer. His phrases are gusts of poetry, buffeting me from every direction. Revelations and admonitions follow upon one another in such rapid succession as to allow me little chance to respond to either. It leaves me feeling alone and sublime and bewildered, as if stranded on a peak somewhere, with the universe at my feet.

When Gurudev speaks of love and surrender, they seem to be inseparable realities. Sometimes he even employs them as interchangeable terms. It reminds me of the ancient symbol of yin–yang, where the black and white portions of a circle curve into one another, each containing a smaller circle of the opposite color. I personally view love as a healthy, positive approach to life; but Guruji is pointing out that at its heart is the unconditional receptivity called surrender. And surrender in Guruji's view is only possible from a positive, courageous impulse of love. It is an attractive mystery. I hope there will be time to explore it further.

An opportunity comes right after our meeting. Sri Sri is accepting private audiences. I get in line and wait, thinking of what to say.

When my turn comes to approach him, my heart is thumping so loudly, I can't even think.

Sri Sri smiles encouragingly.

I blurt out self-consciously that I have been for many years dedicated to teaching the meditation of Maharishi Mahesh Yogi.

With a look of almost pleading, Gurudev responds, "Please don't think of me as separate from him."

Wondering how I can have been so insensitive, I reply in embarrassment, "Oh, no, of course not! You are all One!" I know this intellectually, but, regrettably, have never given much thought to how an enlightened master might *feel* toward others like himself.

Sri Sri somehow orients to my awkward apology in a way that puts me more at ease. I tell him, "I am the person who wrote you that note about the prana techniques."

He smiles with a twinkle and says, "I know,"—as if we are sharing a secret.

I continue, "When you told me to sit and surrender in love, did you mean that that is the next step for me in my spiritual growth?"

His smile and his voice become soft and eager as he says, "Yes, yes."

By now I am looking into his eyes, which welcome me warmly without reservation. "For some reason," I confide, "that scares me. Could it be that I am just not quite ready for it yet, that I should kind of hold off on that until I feel a little more comfortable with it?"

"No no," he says. "You are ready, right now." Holding my gaze, he lights up a playful, twinkling, affectionate smile. "The reason you feel afraid is just …you don't know what will happen!" His smile broadens into silent laughter.

Something shifts inside of me. Suddenly I rather like the prospect of not knowing what will happen, especially if it is going to happen in the company of this gentle soul whose laughing eyes are regarding me so warmly. I sense the workings of a quiet alchemy between us, transforming my fear and anxiety into childlike feelings of excitement and anticipation.

Eagerly, I venture another question: "I do feel attracted to several different masters I have met, and please don't call me a collector this time."

His grin becomes distinctly mischievous.

"No, seriously," I plead. "These attractions come from my heart, and I want to know how to handle them. You say no master would ever feel jealous, but is there any other kind of conflict that could arise? Should I surrender to whomever is given to me at the time? Is there any difficulty if there is more than one?"

"There is no conflict," he replies. "But you should choose one, for the cultivation of your heart." Then with that mischievous grin again, "It doesn't have to be me!" By the end of the phrase he is laughing,—such generous, open-hearted laughter as seems to embrace the universe in total enjoyment and affection.

My inner shift becomes a landslide. I can no longer meet the gaze of his eyes so vibrant with love and delight. I seem to be in the presence of an ancient Being who is offering me what I secretly yearn for more than anything in all of space and time. I feel myself blushing as it dawns on me how totally he is penetrating my truth.

From an impulse of wonderment, I summon the courage to re-encounter his gaze,—emerging into a power of quietness from which every reservation is banished. Out of the soft, mysterious depths of nowhere, something indescribably beautiful opens up for me. All I can think is that I want to spend forever in this whirling magic circle of yin -yang, love and surrender, him and me.

At the opposite end of the room, fellow seekers await their turn.

I press my palms together in the traditional gesture of Namaste, hear myself say "Jai Guru Dev," and nearly lose my balance stepping backward to take my leave. An enormous smile saturates every layer of my life. My heart is dancing like a child. Everything looks so beautiful, so tender, so priceless, so Divine... Reluctant to encounter other eyes, I steal away to a secluded area of the grounds and find a spot under a tree where I become lost in a pool of teardrops and stillness for an unaccountable length of time.

The next day is the last day of our course. A table is put out with a display of items that may be purchased. A picture of Gurudev catches my eye, sending a pang through my heart, reminding me of her newest secret. I purchase the picture, along with a collection of books and tapes.

This evening's meeting is to be our final time with Guruji before his return to India. I love our evening meetings, which are devoted primarily to chanting and dancing. The chants come from various monastic and mystical traditions. Some of them are quite sophisticated, involving regulation of the breath and the effects of sound resonance upon the system. And dancing affords an opportunity for self-expression that feels wonderful after hours of sitting in meditation.

As Guruji walks toward the door at the end of the evening, we are all reluctant to leave him. Somehow, he ends up outside with us in a big circle under the light of a bright full moon. He takes the opportunity to make one more personal connection with each of us, by walking around inside the circle as we gently sway and sing.

Seeing him approach me, I become silent and fold my hands in the gesture of Namaste. He gives me a look and says, "Sing, sing." Of all things, he wants to hear me sing! I timidly pick up the tune, *"Shri Radhe, Radhe, Radhe Shyam..."*—a chant about the ardent yearning of the soul for the infinite love of the Divine Personality. My heart shyly enters my voice as I blend in with the surrounding melody; and Guruji blesses me with another of his wonderful, playful, laughing smiles.

After the flurry of fond farewells and packing and last minute sight-seeing, I confide to my husband, sitting next to me, as our home-bound jet soars skyward: "I feel like I have just embarked upon the ultimate adventure of my life."

Ananda Mouse

Chapter Two

WILDFLOWER IN A HAYFIELD

For years, I have enjoyed listening to inspirational audio-tapes as part of my morning routine. Now, since my return from California, I find that my little collection of Sri Sri Ravi Shankar tapes has completely upstaged all of my old favorites. And my especial favorite among these is a recording, which someone very kindly has given me, of the question and answer discussions from the retreat that I have just personally attended.

My infatuation is obvious. I decide not to resist, and fondly relive the compelling moments of my encounter with Guruji over and over and over again. It seems I can never grow weary of his insights and his teachings. The deeper they penetrate my being, the more enthralled I become. Gurudev's words, re-echoing in my heart and mind, behave like little time-release bullets of wisdom, setting off sporadic internal explosions of insight and self-discovery, shifting and changing my inner and outer terrain. It is as if the "inner game of Russian roulette" has taken on a life of its own, and continues to hold me under its spell, even here at home.

Some of the things that Guruji says about God particularly fascinate me, because of their haunting similarity to

Christ's famous parable about the lilies of the field:

Consider the lilies of the field, how they grow;
They toil not, neither do they spin:
And yet I say unto you,
That even Solomon in all his glory was not arrayed like
one of these.
Wherefore, if God so clothe the grass of the field,
Which today is, and tomorrow is cast into the oven,
Shall he not much more clothe you,
O ye of little faith?

(Matthew 6: 28-30)

These verses charm and puzzle me from early childhood. I am charmed by the image they evoke in my mind—of contentedly basking in the sunshine, like a wildflower in a hayfield, while an extravagant Heavenly Father expresses His love and affection by lavishly adorning me in glorious dresses. But I am puzzled by how such imagery seems so outrageously contradictory to the lessons that I know my parents and Sunday School teachers really want me to learn. The fascinating parable delights my heart to this day, as the inspiration for one of my childhood's secret fantasies about God. But I have to wonder how the values of the Protestant work ethic ever have come to be derived from such poetical lore!

At some point during high school, I adopt an Islamic proverb:

"Trust in Allah, but tie your camel!"

This seems a lot closer to what my childhood preceptors intend to teach me, except for two important considerations: Number one, it comes from a religion they would call heathen, which appeals to the covertly rebellious mood that dominates my adolescent years. And number two, it contains an element of humor, which I like a lot better than the stern seriousness typical of the Protestant attitude, at least as I understand it.

In adulthood, I find myself reading books, listening to tapes, attending seminars, and joining support groups in pursuit of a more spiritually accurate attunement to the universal laws of prosperity. I am certainly contributing to the personal prosperity of several inspirational authors and motivators, and sincerely believe that each one of them is valuable to me in some way. But I cannot honestly point to any particularly tangible or concrete results from all of this rather frenetic inner and outer endeavor. Whichever guidelines I apply, the task of correlating the spiritual and material dimensions of life always seems awkward to me— like trying to put together pieces that come from different puzzles.

Gurudev's words on the subject, parts of his answers to different questions that come up during the course, strike many familiar chords:

"Your fear inside that you may not have enough money, or you will not make enough money, or it will be insufficient, you will be impoverished, attracts such situations around you.

"Look from the past: Have you not been provided? Whenever money was needed, it was there, available for you. You were not starving. I tell you, you will not starve. Don't be afraid.

"But don't just sit and daydream, 'OK, money will come, somebody will come and give me some.' That will not happen either. Get onto your feet. Don't be lazy. And know you will be provided."

"You think God does not know, doesn't care for you? Now look, you have a child in the home, and see how much you care for the child, how much love you have for the child. You think the Divine is less loving? Less loving than you? A million times more love to you!

"All your relationships are just to give you a little taste of what that infinite love is, what that unconditional love is. You love your husband, wife, boyfriend, girlfriend. How much you are attached to them! How much you give yourself to them! You think the Divine is less beloved to you than that?

"The Divine does everything for you and still hides behind you, so that you feel more comfortable. You know? Say suppose I lend you a guitar, and I make you aware that I have lent my guitar to you every day. You don't enjoy having that guitar. But I lend it to you and make you forget you have taken it from me, make you feel that it is your own guitar, you enjoy it more.

"Same way, the Divine has given you the whole world, all the relations, father, mother, brother, sister, boyfriend, girlfriend, husband, wife, enemies, fighters, people who press your buttons. It's such a big gift from all sides, makes you experience all the beautiful flavors in life—sweet, sour, hot, Mexican food, everything.

"Such a love, such a tremendous amount of love!"

His casual, extemporaneous style gives me the impression that Guruji is just taking all of my various puzzle pieces and playfully tossing them up into the air. A configuration emerges, however, enticing me into contemplation:

The dominant theme of an infinitely loving and attentive Divinity is very much the same as in my old favorite Christian parable. But there is also quite a lot of gently humorous pragmatism, similar to my Islamic proverb. And Guruji's statement, "Your fear inside that you may not have enough money...creates such situations around you," distinctly reminds me of the stern causality characteristic of my worry-oriented Protestant upbringing, except that the logic is upside down: Worry and fear are not practical virtues in Guruji's perspective;—as, of course, they also are not in the New Age paradigms to which I currently subscribe.

The only difference is that, somehow, Gurudev's playfully haphazard rendition of the choices and guidelines for correlating spiritual and material life makes everything seem so obvious and simple. Its innocent elegance is breath-taking. The more deeply I ponder, the more perfect and beautiful and easy its message seems to be.

And the lessons in it are poignantly relevant to my current reality.

A major challenge facing me since our retreat is my husband's response to his week with Sir Sri. As the household bookkeeper I conclude, on the basis of careful calculation, that our trip to California is the last major expense our budget can sustain until certain obligations can be retired. Then as soon as we get home, my husband proceeds to quit his job.

To all appearances, I am married to a charming, old-fashioned gentleman who opens doors and carries heavy bags for me, and believes that as a man he should support his wife. Twelve years of marriage, however, have left me under no illusions about the fact that my husband is a man who is never fully identified with any of the roles he plays. Although I am not exactly prepared for it, on the other hand it doesn't entirely surprise me that the liberating influence of Gurudev should motivate him to abruptly bale out of a stifling occupational dead end. It is just that, from my point of view, his timing could hardly be worse.

Our resources are slim indeed. As our debts mount and creditors grow irate, my comfort zone becomes challenged beyond endurance. I turn all of our financial records over to my husband and throw myself into the development of my own fledgling career in the field of educational body-work.

I feel a little guilty abandoning my dear mate to the jaws of creditors and tax officials. But interestingly enough, he seems to be actually thriving in his hostile new domain. There is more color in his cheeks and sparkle in his eyes than I have seen in years. Even our friends remark on it. In effect, my petulant abdication of responsibility serves to empower him, as he wins for himself, from all those hostile telephone voices, the time and respect he needs to explore new vocational possibilities.

Pondering Guruji's teachings in the context of these circumstances, it deeply comes home to me that my own responsible fears and worries about money have probably been for years more damaging to our interests than my husband's current madcap plunge into uncharted financial waters. The clear light of Gurudev's simple, playful wisdom opens me up to some soberingly acute perceptions of myself. I begin to see how from childhood I have chosen to construct a personal belief system centered upon lack-generating attitudes and negative emotions, in spite of the fact that my own favorite scriptures have always beckoned me toward higher values of faith and trust and love.

Returning in mind to the parable of Christ, I see it through fresh eyes. The puzzling contradictions have completely vanished:

Wildflowers aren't lazy, they are just being natural. They are living the lives that are given to them, simple lives of surrender to the grace and wisdom of God. In this, they give company to the greatest of saints and sages.

And as I hearken, day after day, to Guruji's strange answer in response to my question about jealous Divinities, it begins to unfold a compelling relevance for me:

"When you are surrendered, you become so powerful, even more powerful than any angel. When you live that state of love, all the angels and gods, all the beings, come to serve you. You have nothing to do, nothing to get from them. No need to take knowledge or wisdom from anybody, even the angels. Nor wealth from the Goddess of Wealth."

Gurudev, like Christ, is singing the glories of living like a wildflower! To be sure, his words point to a level of reality far beyond my childhood fantasies about being Divinely adorned in glorious dresses. But I feel very much like a child as I glimpse the vastness of these new horizons.

"You have come alone on this planet, haven't you? And you will go alone. Just remember this. You have come alone, and you will go alone. What do you need here? What is it you want here, thirty-forty years when you are here? Can you be just happy?"

His simple questions haunt me, like the faint rhythms of some immortal music, echoing through the hollows of my mind, resonating in the chambers of my heart, sending tremors of recognition through the innermost fibers of my being.

Forty years of feverishness are being shaken out of my life like autumn leaves, as my soul returns to learning her lessons from the innocent elegance of a wildflower in a hayfield.

Chapter Three

HURT IS A PART OF LOVE

Gurudev's Question Basket discourses explore the connection between love and pain as a recurrent theme. When people write questions like, "What can you tell me to make it easier to forgive those people who have hurt me?" or, "Can you say how one learns to love a parent who has hurt oneself very deeply?"—his answers are almost unvaryingly similar:

"If someone has hurt you, it's because they are ignorant that they are hurting you. And it is because you love them. Your hurt is because of your love. Remember this… hurt is because there is love. Hurt is a part of love. Take it as a part of love. That is the way to heal it…

"And if somebody is hurting you or has hurt you, it's because they are hurt. They have a deeper wound. It's just a smell of it coming to you. You can only have compassion toward them. They have no intention to hurt you, number one. And when they have done something that has hurt you, it is because you have loved them deeply. Love carries hurt as its part. It's part of love…

"Someone whom you love, even if they don't smile at you, you get hurt. Small things make you hurt. A word maybe, a slip of tongue, some word they have said—they don't even mean it—that can go deep and hurt you.

"Hurt is an intense sensation. Take it as an intense sensation. Pain is an intense sensation. Observe it… Be natural. Take it for granted that nobody is willing to hurt you. That is how you live in the light of knowledge."

Reflecting upon Guruji's discourses, inwardly fondling his phrases and examples, I sense that this theme holds some special significance for me, and find myself wandering in memory through the many loves that have given shape to my life.

My earliest memory of falling in love takes me to about age three or four, soon after my second sister is born. My relationship with my first sister, who is only seventeen months younger than I am, has become an unmitigated disaster. Her presence in our family seems to make almost everything about me appear unacceptable to our parents.

This happens innocently enough, I suppose, from our parents feeling the need to attend to the practical demands of the increasing population in their home. When I make noise, it happens to be when my baby sister is sleeping, so I get shushed and admonished not to wake her up. When I start to cry, it seems to my parents like a good opportunity to suggest that I ought to consider myself too big for crying, now that there is a baby in the house to take over that privilege. And so on. I really don't understand how or why, but somehow a family pattern emerges, wherein I tend to get cast in the role of the villain, presumed to be the guilty party in every conflict.

It is painful to see how my parents are with their new baby, in contrast to how they are relating to me. But if I express my feelings about this, it only serves to compound the parental disapproval that is coming my way. I feel intensely jealous of my baby sister, and at the same time I understand that jealousy is a "bad little girl" way to feel. I don't see how I can help feeling the way I feel, and it infuriates me to be condemned for it. But I understand that anger is another sinful feeling, even more certain to provoke censure. There seems to be no way out of my own smoldering internal conflict, which begins to generate a self-assessment tinged by despair.

Into this thoroughly miserable time of my life comes my second little sister. I am big enough now to be allowed to hold her and rock her and help keep her entertained. Even though she is a baby, it is obvious how much she likes me to play with her. Her innocent responses of trust and belonging and affection evoke corresponding feelings in my own heart. I find happiness in her company. Naturally, I begin to rely upon her for soothing respite from the torment of my other family relationships.

It isn't long before my heart is responding to the opportunity to flow again with a torrent of passionate enthusiasm. My little baby sister becomes the original heroine of my life. I appreciate that she has literally rescued me from an emotional dungeon, and my adoration for her knows no bounds. Even though she is three years younger than me,

I see her as gifted with some kind of special grace that makes her superior to other mortals. Miraculously, she never disillusions my mind or betrays my trust. Even into adulthood, the bond between her and me endures as one of the emotional anchors of my life.

My relationships with my parents and first sister continue to be stormy, and there are still plenty of incidents requiring me to contend with all that pain. But an angel of sunshine has arisen in my sky, and a few thunderclouds here and there really do not matter so much anymore.

Having discovered the magic of falling in love, my heart does not stop with just my baby sister. In subsequent years of childhood, similar bondings spring up with a favorite cousin, several best girlfriends, a dear aunt, and certain very special teachers. Every heart-throb becomes an adventure, as I enter the inner and outer world of my beloved via that uncritically open receptivity which is unique to the infatuated state.

Some of my heart's most exhilarating thrills overtake me in relationships with teachers. I have the good fortune to grow up in a community where education is highly valued. There are sensitive and cultivated people standing in front of certain classrooms. As I fall in love with them, their assignments become effortless ecstasy for me. They in turn perceive me as being unusually gifted, often going out of their way to cultivate my talents and abilities. Altogether, it makes for a wonderfully rich educational experience.

As I ponder the loves of my heart, it occurs to me that I am a rather well nourished individual. This is a startling thought. I have a life-long habit of regarding myself with certain misgivings. The "bad little girl" of my early childhood grows up and studies psychology and recovers a reasonably healthy level of self-esteem. But I continue to regard myself as somewhat compromised emotionally by the early estrangement between myself and my parents and first sister.

Now suddenly I see how this very estrangement is instrumental in broadening my horizons from an early age. It teaches me to appreciate the value of friendship and love wherever it is to be found, and motivates me to find it almost everywhere I go. My life-long curse begins to seem more like a life-long blessing!

I think of my first sister. I am breaking an inner taboo against even holding her in my thoughts. It takes a conscious effort, and feels a little spooky, like opening a dusty padlocked door into a long-forbidden room:

My first sister stays emotionally close to our parents all her life. She marries a clergyman of the same religious persuasion they espouse. She gives them four grandsons to continue to dote upon. They live just far enough apart for visits to feel like special events, yet close enough to spend time together almost on a monthly basis. They often take long-distance vacations together. Their mutual enjoyment is deep and genuine.

I notice that I am actually contemplating these scenes without anger, and without my habitual feelings of jealousy. For the first time in my life, I am able to appreciate that the love between my sister and our parents is a beautiful thing. In fact, I feel grateful to her for enriching their lives in so many ways. I could never do as much for them. My heart and mind require unfettered freedoms, which would be impossible within the confines of their fundamentalist beliefs.

My thoughts turn to my parents. Their courtship is conducted almost entirely through overseas letters during World War II. My father is just returned from four years of active military duty. My mother is a thousand miles away from her childhood home for the first time in her life. In pictures from this era, they look like young teenagers. On their wedding day, Mom is, in fact, barely twenty. It is a time of major transition for both of them when I, as their first child, enter into their lives, less than a year into their marriage. I can hardly fault them for being perhaps not quite emotionally ready to contend with the unrelenting demands of a newborn child.

By the time my first sister comes along, Mom and Dad are a lot more settled into their life together, and better equipped to savor the joys of new parenthood. The differences I so painfully perceive between the way they relate to me, and the way they relate to my sister, are definitely not imaginary. But I cannot begrudge them the enjoyment of love as and when it is emotionally possible for them. They do their honest best with me; and in between the gaps, Divine Providence never fails to supply me with love and nurture in all the special flavors most ideally suited to the uniqueness that is me.

A scene comes to my mind, of my mother... She and my sister and I get caught up in one of our bitter spats in the kitchen, which is where they usually happen.

I trek out into the woods to soothe my wounded feelings. I love the woods. The creek and the trees, the squirrels and the wildflowers, somehow give me a sense of belonging, even when I feel rejected by members of my family. I have a fantasy of being a wild creature myself, mistakenly transplanted into a domestic environment.

I return to my bedroom and curl up with a favorite book. Romantic novels provide another escape route into fantasy; and fantasy serves the vital function of keeping my heart alive when reality lets me down.

My mother is knocking on my bedroom door. Reluctantly, I answer. She opens the door, apologizes for some of her harsh words, and gives me a hug. She actually does this more than once. It takes a lot of courage, because I am not particularly responsive to her overtures. I feel there are too many things about me that she can't approve of or, perhaps, even understand; and I just can't open up to her. She knows she has lost touch with me, and can't find how to mend the broken bond. These are painful moments for both of us.

In my heart I know that there is a deep and abiding love between my parents and myself. We continue to keep in touch even though the estrangement between us is felt on both sides over many years. Gurudev is so right: The hurt is there because the love is there. This is one of the primordial truths of my life.

I think of Guruji's words about jealousy, and my futile attempt to see my first sister as part of myself in the dinner table scenario. His instruction to "make a flower bunch" comes up in my mind. Idly, I begin to play with it: What kind of "flower bunch" are my family and me?

In my mind's eye, I see myself in relation to my family as a colorful wild rose adding interest to a lovely garden bouquet. There are some thorns that are a part of me, but actually that's okay: Even they have roles to play in bringing out the passionate and tender beauty of the whole.

Chapter Four

NEW VESSELS FOR NEW WINE

Predisposed as I am to personal habits of self-reflection and contemplation, I cannot help noticing how some of my most negative and limiting internal self-images are rapidly losing credibility. Poverty consciousness and emotional woundedness are two internal monsters that have been haunting me for years, and I have expended enormous effort in attempting to overcome them. Now I find them literally wilting out of my life, in response to a few playful darts from this disarmingly child-like saint. And new self-images are springing up almost magically to take their place, requiring no effort whatever in the way of visualization or auto-suggestion.

Being a wildflower in a hayfield, and a wild rose in a garden bouquet, transforms my internal terrain dramatically. I begin to feel almost helplessly wealthy and well-nourished as I move through my daily life. Personal compliments are raining down on me from every direction—friends, clients, colleagues, even my family! Have I walked into a fairly tale, or what?

In any case, my experience is that I have come into an unexpected and gratifying personal inheritance. Gurudev, seeing my stores of wealth, has led me to the hidden keys.

Now the doors of my storehouses are open, and the question is coming up in my mind of how to best employ my expanded resources. As I think about this, another phrase of his bedazzling response to my question about jealous Divinities, begins to convey significance:

"You have come here to give something, contribute something. Whatever you could do to people, do it, from your side. Finished. Very simple."

I know that it is the dharma of the wealthy to give. But I wonder if Guruji means that there is something in particular I am supposed to be contributing here on this planet—something that perhaps I ought to be getting on with. What might it be that I am "here to give?" Could it be something I am, at least to some extent, already doing? Maybe. But then why would Gurudev bring it up so pointedly? Somehow, I have the feeling that he wants to effect some shift in the direction that my activities and contributions are taking. But where from, and where to?

Guruji isn't the first person ever to tell me that I have something to offer. In fact, I have been hearing this since childhood. Like many over-achieving eldest siblings, I win acclaim as a gifted student, score highly in intelligence and aptitude, and sail through most of my education on a full mast of honors and scholarships. My adult accomplishments, however, are modest. In general, I gravitate toward small-time leadership positions or independent endeavors.

Maybe Guruji is simply saying the same thing as all my

earlier teachers: 'God has given you a lot in the way of talents and abilities, and expects a lot from you in return.' Dutifully, I begin to think in terms of assuming some leadership responsibility or initiating some new enterprise in the cause of Sri Sri's Art of Living Foundation. But I detect a certain weariness in my heart around thoughts of this kind, which makes me pause. I sense that there is a kind of new wine flowing in my life, for which the old familiar vessels feel oddly inadequate.

Listening again to my audiotape from Sri Sri's retreat, I notice his response to someone's question about how to offer service:

"Dearest Gurudev,

"In thinking about service to humanity, I always return to the same question. I am on a spiritual path myself and contributing to raising world consciousness on the individual level, but on the level of activity, where does one start to help? Drug addiction, chronic welfare dependency, environmental hazards, AIDS, etc. How can one really make a difference? Sometimes helping others to help themselves isn't easy. They are not always open to help. Can you comment, please? Is any one of the problems more important, more basic, than the others?"

Guruji's answer, as usual, shifts me inward: "See, service—first you understand this: it is not an action, it is an attitude. Your willingness to serve—when the time comes, you will jump into it. Whatever is needed, whenever it is needed, and however your service is needed, you will jump into it.

"Otherwise, you fix in your mind, 'OK, my service is what? To take care of these hospital things, or to take care of the homeless.' And now you are narrowed. It has become just another job for you. Now someone asks you a small favor: 'Can you please take my bag and leave it in the other room?' You will say, 'No, I am sorry. I am busy.' That is no service.

"Service, now see this: that very attitude in you, willing to be... You know, to someone whom you love, you say, 'I am here for you. If you need anything, I am here. If you need me, please tell me. I am here, ready there, for you.' Say that to everybody. 'If you need me, I am here.' You say to your children, or your husband, your wife, or your parents, or your very close, loved people, 'I am here for you. If you need anything, please tell me.' Many of you tell me, 'If you need anything...' So tell this to everybody. This is real service.

"I'm not saying not to be discrete in doing your service. OK, say, 'I am here for everybody,' and someone comes, 'OK, then you close your bank account, put all the money in my bank account.' That is not it.

"You see, willingness to serve, willingness to serve, and then doing it."

Gurudev's critique is true of me. Much of my productive time is spent in service to enlightened causes, and it is frequently "a job" for me. The "attitude" of service is also present, to varying degrees at different times. But the sense of identifying a particular service as my chosen domain definitely predominates. In this approach to service, and in spite of my best intentions, I often get drawn into competitive, rather than cooperative, interactions with other people. And when such competitive feelings come up, I do experience feeling "narrowed," as Guruji describes.

But it has never occurred to me that the narrowing actually begins in the intellectual process of choosing a particular domain of service. It is an intriguing insight. I decide to consciously try out Gurudev's suggestion—to take the attitude of 'I am here for you,' and wait and see what sort of needs might come beckoning to me.

It isn't long before an aggressively networking friend tells me she is recommending me to Guruji for the leadership position of Facilitator in our local Art of Living center. I assure her I will be glad to do it. Interestingly enough, nothing ever comes of this.

Meanwhile, my promiscuous heart is busy falling in love again,—this time with *bhajans*, the Indian devotional chanting which Guruji recommends for use in our weekly meetings. In the process of collecting tapes and tracking down text, I find myself in the company of several similarly infatuated enthusiasts. We meet together in twos and threes to practice the songs, master the art of "bliss-building" sequences, and generally conspire over ways to "turn on" the rest of our group.

One of our strategies is to put out song sheets to help people learn the chants more easily. One evening as I am handing out song sheets, someone very warmly thanks me for the helpful service. It feels so strange. In my enthusiasm for this music, I have no concept that I am engaged in service. I feel more like I am conspiring to tempt others into the enjoyment of a seductive pleasure. My Protestant conscience can hardly condone the idea that something so fun, and so sensually delightful, should be given such a virtuous credential!

On the other hand, is this perhaps what Gurudev means when he says that service is simply being there for people, whatever the need? Some people do feel a need for song sheets; and here we are, handing them out. We don't seem to be drawing very heavily upon the more intense virtues such as dedication, commitment, responsibility, etc., which I customarily associate with doing service. But our actions do appear to fit the master's simple criteria.

As I look around at my life from this perspective, I notice that there are several more places where a similar phenomenon is cropping up. In the actual singing of the bhajans, for example: My enthusiasm plus a little bit of musical background quickly transforms me into one of the more competent singers. But I rarely choose to be the one to lead the chants. This is not entirely out of shyness. In fact, I have a fair amount of experience leading things; and it is often my personal tendency to stand up and take charge. However, we have several good bhajan leaders; and what seems to be more needed is for other strong singers to pick up their cue and keep the musical momentum going. Pragmatically, I find myself gravitating toward this secondary role just because it is a lot more fun to sing a bhajan that picks up and moves along. But hidden within this practical consideration, I detect another little sprout of the "I am here for you" feeling in my heart.

In my marriage, work, and family relationships, also, I am experiencing more of an attraction to support roles, and less of my usual inclination to take the lead. I'm becoming more a behind-the-scenes facilitator, and less a front-and-center personality. In fact, the practice of being "here for you" seems to be shifting my entire interpersonal life into subtler realms of orientation. The attentive, intuitive process of sensing where something is needed and feeling out how to offer that particular kind of help or support, quietly draws me into the company of other people who sense or feel the same needs; and these companionships naturally unfold into mutual collaboration for effecting practical solutions.

True, there are occasional awkward moments and false starts as I explore this new approach. But the overall adventure is seductively charming. And the experiences of friendship and camaraderie that tend to flourish around it are becoming so precious to my heart! For so many years I have been dogged by feelings of loneliness while almost single-handedly starting and leading centers for meditation and self-development. Even though the people who take advantage of my services often become genuine friends, they also tend to relate to me rather as representing a cause, than as a simple fellow sojourner. Now these old familiar feelings of isolation and competitiveness, so frustratingly associated with service in worthy causes, seem to be fading out of my life. Coming up in their place are nurturing interactions full of warmth and amicability, light-heartedness and intimacy. Everywhere it touches my life, "I am here for you" is gently opening the doors of heart to heart.

It occurs to me that I am actually learning the ropes of yet another "inner game." You could call it the "inner game of service," with Gurudev's "I am here for you" being the key to how to play it. And some of its rules are clearly non-negotiable.

I am learning that "I am here for you" is one of those things that has to be kept simple: If I complicate it, it won't work. "I am here for you" cannot be employed as a logical, intellectual position. It's not a head thing. Trying to make it intellectual is likely to lead into exploitative relationships, as in Guruji's example of "OK, then you close your bank account and put all the money into my bank account."

"I am here for you" is also not an ego-identification. I am learning that if I let my ego get hooked into it, I may find myself caught up in some grandiose, co-dependent fantasy of heroic rescue or quixotic crusade. "Like a bridge over troubled waters, I will lay me down," as the song goes.

Emotionally charged and ego-soaring inspirations toward self-sacrifice may make for stirring music, but they often become sadly dysfunctional in practical life.

In the true Zen spirit of moderation, "I am here for you" proves in action to be neither an ego trip, nor a head trip. As Guruji describes, it is simply "an attitude, willingness to serve." An *attitude* is of the heart. Willingness to serve seems truly to be one of the most natural and spontaneous impulses of the human heart.

I realize now that Gurudev himself is being "here for me" by not acting on my friend's recommendation that he make me one of his organizational leaders. Such a position would almost certainly draw me back into old patterns, leaving me less free to discover and explore these new directions which are so nourishing to my soul. Indeed, as it turns out, Guruji's words of advice are effecting a significant change in the direction of my personal contributions. Through the gentle art of being "here for you," both my leadership and my supportive roles are being remarkably transformed.

But best of all is the wonderful, relaxed openness that pervades my life these days. In the pleasure gardens of her Beloved, the revelry of my soul continues to distil exhilarating variations upon the wine of life and love. Their enjoyment charms me increasingly into new activities and unfamiliar roles, as the Divine Potter, sitting at the wheel of time, turns out the suitable vessel for each distinctively flavored brew. I perceive that in this process, my life is being gently coaxed out of its old stagnant ruts and into fresh new pastures of challenge, growth and adventure.

Chapter Five

SANDCASTLES OF IDENTITY

It is nearly a year and a half before Sri Sri Ravi Shankar returns to North America. In the meantime, I take advantage of opportunities to visit other touring saints, and participate in seminars offered by several inspirational personalities. I find these to be lovely and uplifting experiences. But my heart and my mind keep returning to Sri Sri's knowledge, Sri Sri's practices, Sri Sri's wisdom. It is obvious that Gurudev's presence in my inner life has grown to almost mythical proportions. I wonder what it would be like to actually see him again.

It excites me to learn that Sri Sri is offering a Midwest retreat this year. It is scheduled to take place during July at an outdoor conference center on the scenic shores of Lake Geneva in Southeastern Wisconsin. However, our finances are still a little shaky, and my husband and I cannot quite afford the cost for both of us to attend.

Someone offers me the option of helping with childcare in return for limited course participation. I have very little experience with children, along with feelings of incompetence due to my inability to have my own. But the offer makes it possible for my husband to enroll in the course, and for both of us to spend a week with Guruji. I push my self-doubts aside and accept the position.

I vaguely presume that the "inner game of Russian roulette" will have limited sway over me while I am manning a service role that limits direct exposure to Sri Sri himself, but this assumption is almost immediately challenged. On the first day of the retreat, one of the parents asks Guruji, "What are the three most important things we should teach our children?" He answers that "there are three most important things we all need to learn from children: innocence, belonging, and being in the moment."

At the time of this exchange, I am not even present in the room. I am out rounding up child-size tables and chairs. Nevertheless, when it is repeated to me, my guts register an uncanny intuition that Gurudev's words contain a message for me. I hear myself laughing, just as everyone else must have laughed, over the master's gentle exposure of the well-meaning arrogance of parenthood. But underneath my laughter I sense an internal repositioning, a shifting and sharpening of my awareness. I recognize an echo from my own childhood—the words of Christ upon a similar theme:

"...of such is the Kingdom of God.

Verily, I say unto you,

Whosoever shall not receive the Kingdom of God as a little child,

He shall not enter therein."

Mark 10:14-15

Up to this moment, my mind has been preoccupied with the practical aspects of the responsibility I am undertaking. I am intent upon doing my best with an unfamiliar task. Our childcare team has met several times to prepare for the retreat; and it reassures me to know that we are well-equipped with games, art supplies, and structured schedules for filling up the half-dozen summer days ahead.

Now all of that suddenly seems superficial. Guruji's words remind me that my reason for being here is not so much to teach and offer guidance, as to learn and receive guidance. My apprehensions about being somewhat out of place in childcare give way to thoughtful reflections upon how appropriate the assignment actually seems to be. I hear about innocence, belonging, and being in the moment nearly every day at home as I listen to Sri Sri's audiotaped discourses. I find it charming that such warm, light-hearted virtues should receive so much emphasis in his teachings. But I am also aware that innocence, belonging, and being in the moment are not, as of yet, fully functional components of my character.

It is said that there will be wisdom and higher purpose behind anything that happens in the vicinity of the Enlightened. I can see how, if I were to find myself sitting at the feet of the Master among the rest of the adults, it might only re-enforce my ivory-tower tendency to merely contemplate his teachings and then mentally archive them, like museum pieces in my private collection. Maybe what I need at this time is more along the lines of role-modeling, to help me translate this wisdom into the actions and habit patterns of everyday living.

Never mind that my designated role models are nearly all less than half as tall as me. Under the bodhi-tree of Gurudev's darshan, they demonstrate beyond all doubt their mastery of the arts I am assigned to learn from them, —immersing me in a world of little hands and little feet, trusting eyes and soft shy hugs, eager displays of pebble collections and captured bugs, instant tears, unbridled laughter, outbursts of temper forgotten within minutes, boundless energy, silly squabbles, naïve mischief, and a general flow of event and emotion so changeable as to leave scarcely a trace from one moment to the next. No doubt, the parents who are enrolled in Sri Sri's retreat are grateful for the chance to get away from all this for a few days of adult peace and quiet. But for me it is a poignant journey into a long-forgotten world.

The practical content of my activities with the children ranges from ordinary to mundane: Find what happened to the green paint, sort out whose turn it is to swim with the inner tube… And yet, I could hardly ask for a more tangible, interactive demonstration of the values of child-like spirituality. As I respond to the wide bright eyes and little pointing fingers that petition me for help with opening cans of play dough, waves of relaxation flow softly through my heart. The children's simple trust in me is even more reassuring than the friendly encouragement of the fellow adults with whom I share this task.

It is the children who possess the natural courage to take the emotional initiative. My heart is gratefully, often almost shyly, following their lead. Children seldom doubt their emotions, and in their company it seems pointless to doubt my own. It is amazing how easily the infectious naiveté of childhood can erode my grown-up barriers and reserves. Sometimes I wonder what might happen if they were to catch on to the fact that I am probably learning a lot more from them than they could possibly be learning from me. And sometimes I feel convinced that in fact they know this, to the point of taking it completely for grant-ed. Often they seem truly to be little sages, patiently or impatiently humoring the limitations of their adult atten-dants.

In fact, being with the children is many ways similar to being in the presence of the master. Intimations of eterni-ty float into our moments like butterflies riding on warm summer breezes. One little girl likes to crawl into my lap, in her wet bathing suit, just for a momentary hug before crawling back down to go play some more in the water. She knows and I know, beyond words, beyond thought, of the purpose and place of love in the universe.

The demands of each day's experiences with the children keep my mind active in attempts to recover the under-standing of what used to be fun and important to me at the age of three or five or six or eight. This stirs up the floodwaters of old memories. Especially during the quiet moments after my morning and evening meditation, scenes and events that I haven't recollected for decades transport me back...into the bright green canopy of leaves I can almost touch with my feet as I soar forward on the swing my father has strung up between the two tall trees on the south side of our house...into the enormous piles of autumn leaves that billow up around me as I plunge down from the lower branches of those same two trees...into the snow on the big hill at Grandma's house where I climb up and slide down all afternoon to the point of delicious exhaustion...into the marshmallows melting on hot chocolate which I sip while decorating Christmas cookies with icing and colored crystals of sugar...into the crazy hilarity of after-dinner tickle-fests with my whole family rolling around on the living room rug like a bunch of puppy-dogs, in silly celebration of the sheer joy of being alive...into the sharing of secrets with my favorite cousin as we pack our lunches and set out on day-long hikes across our fathers' fields and down shady country roads, finding abandoned houses to explore and imagining romantic scenes among the heroes and heroines who once must have lived in them...

This process of reaching back stimulates a lot of emotional release. My nighttime pillows are moistened by softly flowing tears of reunion with the little girl who still lives so innocently deep inside of me, who still takes spontaneous delight in so many things, who still unquestioningly knows how tenderly she is cherished every moment in this world, who is still so very much like the little children I am attending to all day long.

It strikes me that my nocturnal tears are not at all melancholy. On the contrary, I am repeatedly overwhelmed by how rich and beautiful and happy all these childhood memories are. It is so amazing! Most of my adult recollections of childhood tend to focus upon the negative. In psychotherapy, I probe into the anger and fear around my sibling rivalry issues, the competition and distrust between myself and my mother, and so on. In rebirthing I re-live the life-and-death trauma of getting stuck in the birth canal while my mother is under total anesthesia for her final twelve hours of labor. In prosperity support groups I examine the early financial struggles of my family. Even under the influence of Guruji, I am learning to understand and accept the hurt that is part of the love between members of my family and myself.

All of these endeavors do lead me to meaningful resolutions of troublesome issues. Psychotherapy helps me release pent up anger and rebuild self-esteem. Rebirthing results in noticeable relief from certain respiratory problems that plague me since the asthma of my infancy. It is helpful to understand how my parents' financial anxieties still affect the way I relate to money. Learning to accept the pain of love is a tender, ongoing process in my heart. But even though all these insights and resolutions are valuable to my life, the process of pursuing them leaves me with a distanced perception of my childhood, reducing it to a series of struggles and ordeals that I feel like I would never want to have to live through again.

But now, mysteriously, the distance between myself and my childhood is vanishing. It is as if the angels guarding the gates put away their flaming swords and allow me to wander freely back into the garden. And the childhood I am rediscovering almost seems to be a different story. Memory after memory chronicles a history of sunshine and warmth and happiness. Richly fulfilling experiences of love and delight appear, in truth, to be vastly more numerous and predominant than the occasional incidents of suffering that preoccupy most of my adult recollections. It gives me the uneasy feeling that a kind of injustice is being perpetrated within my inner domain. To a disturbing extent, I seem to be falsely conceiving of myself as the survivor of painful and unhappy early years.

While the children around me are sculpting forts and castles from the sand upon the beach, my own sandcastles of self-concept are being eroded and washed away by the irresistible tidewaters of expanding reality. Some kind of internal censorship is being lifted, allowing me freer access to the unabridged version of my own origins. As the reels of memory unroll, many of my habitual notions of how I come to be me, begin to appear lopsided and unsubstantial.

My first sister, for example—the rival sibling I mentally characterize as the nemesis of my youth—how central she is to so many delightful recollections! Being closest to me in age, she is in fact my most constant playmate. We share the same bed from the time she graduates out of the cradle until the time I leave home for college. We borrow each other's clothes, make each other presents, listen to each other's prayers, talk each other to sleep after our parents turn out the light and close our bedroom door. One summer, I actually read the entire text of "Gone with the Wind" to her as we lounge upon our bed after finishing our evening chores. Although it is true that she is never quite as special to my heart as my second sister is, in a practical sense, my first sister and I are actually more intimate. The bitter spats that sometimes arise between us probably account for less than one hour in a thousand over our years of companionship. And yet, my mind fixates upon the pain of these exceptional moments, and all but forgets the far more plentiful pleasures of this extensive and rich relationship.

And the mother who comes back to me now is more like an adorable angel than an object of distrust. She is patiently teaching me to embroider almost before I can talk. She is giving me a little bucket and letting me help her gather the eggs—until it becomes apparent that I am allergic to the dust in the henhouse. She is standing me up on a chair by the counter so I can 'help' her cook our meals. She is letting me poke the bean seeds into the soil of the garden when it would take her half as long by herself. She is finding room in our limited family budget for me to have the music lessons she wishes she could have had as a girl. She is constantly busy with the many chores of the farm, and constantly finding creative ways to include me in every activity. Just about the only time she ever discourages me from learning how to do anything is when I want to be a ballerina, because at the time our family religion still thinks dancing is sinful.

My mother is not an educated woman, being often kept home from school to work in the cotton fields of her family's struggling Texas farmstead. But without a doubt she is deserving of far more credit than I habitually give her for the bright and confident student my subsequent teachers encounter.

It is painful to be re-awakened to so many tender recollections of the very first people my heart learns to regard with caution and reserve. Actually, I feel like caution and reserve may still be appropriate as part of my approach to them. But I also feel a yearning to tear down those barricades and flow with freedom in the waves of tenderness and love that are clearly more true to the story we so intimately share.

I wonder how such frightful barriers come to be erected between us in the first place. How do I come to conceive of my sister as a menacing enemy, my mother as a disapproving judge, and myself as a kind of outlaw, rebelliously opposing or furtively eluding their conspiratorial campaigns against me? In the more fully detailed chronicle to which I am regaining access, fights with my sister and censure from my mother are not even particularly frequent events, and account for only a fraction of what these relationships contribute to my life. Yet they persist as the cornerstones underlying several turrets and gables in my citadel of self-concept, while most of our happy episodes lie obscured among the archives sequestered within its fortified walls.

Thumbing through my mental index in search of relevant wisdom, I recall how Guruji often speaks of the mind as having an inherent bias toward the negative. "If you are given ten compliments," he says, "and one insult, that one insult gets into your mind so strongly, it overwhelms you, it takes you in your totality, it eats you up. All pleasant thoughts leave you. One unpleasant thought clogs the mind, clogs your life, limits it to a very small thing. ...Our mind immediately catches hold of the negative event and goes around with it. Ten positive events, and one negative event is sufficient...ten wonderful days, and one day of misunderstanding, fight, equals it off."

How descriptive this is of myself! A mere handful of negative events certainly appears to be clogging and limiting my life, and over a very long time! During a free moment, I locate one of the many tapes in which Sri Sri discusses this subject, and put it into my Walkman.

"Just look at the things you doubt," he suggests. "What do you doubt in your life? Do you doubt something that is positive, or something that is negative? You'll find that your doubt is always with something that is very positive. You never doubt yourself when you are depressed. Do you ever doubt, 'Am I really depressed?' You never doubt if somebody is angry with you, mad at you. If someone shouts at you, do you question, 'Did you really shout at me? Are you really angry at me?' You don't ask. But if someone says 'I love you,' you ask them 'Do you really love me? Are you sure?' Our doubt is always about something that is positive. Just see. You doubt in the goodness of people, but you never doubt in the badness of people. You take it for granted that they are basically worst, hopeless, bad."

Gurudev's words remind me of the doctrine of innate depravity, which figures prominently in my childhood religious upbringing. My earliest preceptors are dedicated to the idea that even little children are naturally sinful. They hold the belief that every human being, except for Christ himself, is in need of redemption from the moment egg meets sperm. The fact that babies cry is cited as evidence for this assertion. In one of the lovely Christmas carols taught to every child in our church, there is a verse claiming that the infant Jesus, being sinless, never cries.

Even as a child, I suspect an adult agenda behind this teaching, and it doesn't take a lot of education to convince my inquiring mind of its absurdity. Obviously, Guruji hasn't much use for it, either. But he often points out, citing numerous examples, how the mind has a built-in tendency to adopt and build upon such negatively charged conclusions and beliefs. It introduces an intriguing angle on the subject. Evidently there is something more *innate* about the doctrine of innate depravity than I fully comprehend. And evidently that something is also *innate* to the ways of my own mind, deeply influencing some of the directions in which it is guiding my life.

Sri Sri's discussions typically go on to spell out the lesson of how to handle the mind,—first of all, by simply learning to accept it for what it is:

"What is mind? Mind is time, and time is mind… What is it the mind does? It goes either to the past, or to the future. We are angry about the past, or anxious about the future… Our mind is so much used to living in opposite values…

"Trust has its value, so also doubt. Do you see that? …Doubt is a disease, if it is with the positive. Doubt in the negativity in people, in yourself. Doubt in the incapability of you. If you get mad, doubt, 'Am I really angry? No, no, it's just something.' You know, if you are upset, don't believe that you are really upset. 'No, something has happened.' You know? 'It's not my nature.' Don't believe you are an angry person, or you are an unhappy person. Doubt in this negativity in you. Then you will doubt in the negativity of people around you also. A new level in life begins, and fear vanishes from your life. …Place the doubt in the negativity. Place the doubt in the negativity of yourself and people around you. Then trust in your life grows naturally. And trust is innocence. When there is trust, there is no fear in life. Doubt brings along with it fear."

I think of myself as a pretty good student of psychology, applying its principles wisely to my life. But apparently I am also a perfect case in point of Gurudev's critique, and still need to learn how to handle my own mind.

Guruji's examples of how to doubt in the negative rather than the positive put me in mind of my second sister. Perhaps her position in our family enables her to perceive the mistakes the rest of us are making, and choose a wiser course. Or perhaps she really is just naturally gifted with some rare and special grace, as I often imagine. Whatever the reason, all through our youthful years she possesses an almost unconscious talent for conducting her life according to the principles Gurudev is describing. Her immunity to the magnetism of negative turmoil is one of the wonders of my world. Anger, hatred, fear, and jealousy seem like silly nonsense to her. She can look at almost anything that happens and smile with indulgent affection, totally convinced that however misguided any of us might be in the moment, at bottom all we want is to express the love in our hearts.

It charms me like a magic spell. When I get caught up in my recurrent stormy situations, taking refuge in my second sister's comfort is like escaping to an island of sanity: 'I know Mommy doesn't really feel that way. She just kind of loses it sometimes.' 'Daddy is so adorable, even when he gets mad. You can tell how sorry he feels, the very next second. He really couldn't hurt a flea.' 'Of course she loves you. You're her big sister. She just gets frustrated because you are always so good at everything.' Such innocent convictions have the power to enchant and quieten my dubious mind, and my heart clings onto them like precious miracles of wizened driftwood for surviving stormy seas.

My second sister has a passionate and contagious sense of family loyalty, and I am not the only one who feels a special connection with her. She occupies a similar status with both of our other sisters, our two brothers, and our parents, as well as a number of cousins, aunts and uncles.

Then during her college years she commits the unthinkable and becomes pregnant out of wedlock—not intentionally, but this is the sixties, and caution is not the trend of the times. Her boyfriend gallantly offers to pay for an abortion, but that is not what my sister wants her first experience of motherhood to be. Instead, she interrupts her studies and takes a job in a sandwich shop to earn the money she needs to pay the medical expenses of having her baby on her own.

Waves of shock and humiliation sweep through our sheltered and conservative clan. Certain of the more religiously zealous advise our parents that such a daughter ought to be disowned. One of our father's cousins forbids his daughters to have any social contact with her. An in-law aunt refuses to allow her toddler even to come into the same room with the "fallen woman," as if her condition might be contagious. It looks as though we are headed for one of those horror stories of shunning and rejection that have scarred American community life since the era of the Scarlet Letter.

Some of our relatives counsel my sister to discreetly disappear for a few months, and then give up her baby for adoption. In fact, many of them expect her to pursue some such course. But she won't hear of this, either. 'In that case I would never know what is happening to my baby,' she insists. 'With me I know she is loved, and that is the most important thing.'

In the face of her ingenuous persistence, a minor miracle takes place among our kin. Initial reactions are angry and judgmental. But hearts begin to recoil from the harsh cruelty of putting such motives into action, and second thoughts become reflective: 'You know, I can understand the way she feels. It reminds me of my school friend Thelma, in the days of the war, who had a baby by a transient soldier and gave it up for adoption. She's married now and has other children, but she still yearns to know what is happening to her firstborn.'

The situation is intense, especially for our parents, as it dawns on them that their children may be entering a world of values and assumptions shockingly divergent from their own. Their peers, too, begin to realize that similar crises could happen in almost any family "these days;" and expressions of empathy, comfort, and encouragement begin to replace the sterner stuff. My sister discovers that our father's deepest anguish has less to do with issues of propriety and reputation than with the simple fear of losing his daughter's love. Of course she ardently assures him that no such thing is even possible, that regardless of where her life might lead, her love and adoration for him could never diminish for even a minute. Her initiative to keep open the heart lines of communication are enthusiastically seconded by idealistic letters from myself (away in college at the time), arguing that our family's main concern ought to be affirming the new life coming into our midst, and generally expounding upon the theme that 'love is the answer.' My heady and naïve contributions probably are not all that helpful, but I like to think that at least they give another little push to our growing consensus that this is a time for mutual support rather than divisive rejection.

With the approach of her due date, my sister quits her job and moves back home, as the somber and stormy family sentiments quietly shift toward practical and caring acceptance of our bittersweet reality. 'Imagine, another baby in the house, after all these years!' 'Our first grandchild.' 'Do you think we can fix up that old oak high chair? It must be a valuable antique by now.' 'Any child of hers just has to be special.' On my holiday visits, I notice that throughout her pregnancy, my sister keeps a Snoopy card on her dressing table that reads, "Life is One Big Thrill after Another!"

About a year after the birth of her baby daughter, the father outgrows his playboy philosophy and begins to court my sister in earnest. Their happily thriving marriage is now more than two decades old, and their daughter's promising career in the performing arts is a source of pride among all our kin. When anyone in our family even remembers the unconventional beginnings of their story, it is only with the same fond indulgence that my sister always extends to everyone else's foibles and shortcomings. And when family crises arise, it is she, more than anyone else, in whom we all confide.

My second sister exerts a tremendously powerful influence in my life. She establishes her claim to my heart while she is still so small that I can sit in my own child-size rocking chair and hold her in my arms. I am responding to her empathy long before she can put feelings into words. It doesn't matter that she is over three years younger than me. As she grows from infancy into childhood, my gratitude and love for her blossom into ardent adoration, and I find myself aspiring to be like the way she is. As my own horizons expand into realms outside our immediate family, it is my second sister's image and example that guide my course. I feel anxious to avoid any possible recurrence of the problems that mar my original family relationships, and cling to her natural wisdom as a kind of insurance against that danger.

My sister's charmed approach to life never comes quite as naturally to me as it does to her. I have to constantly remind myself of things that she takes completely for granted—that people are basically friendly and will generally welcome me onto their good side. For me, this requires a certain amount of thought. In fact, I have to work at it pretty hard. But my efforts are crowned with success, and lead me into a number of important nurturing relationships.

There is, however, one sphere in which I never can succeed with this approach: Try as I might to adapt my second sister's wisdom to my previously established family relationships, I cannot do it. Even though her natural expressions of innocence and trust and love will always prevail with them, they don't entirely buy into my emulation of her virtues. Instead of understanding and supporting my efforts to relate to them more wisely and lovingly, they tend to view my attempts with distrust, and even sometimes to interpret me as expressing some kind of vaguely disrespectful attitude. My tenuous foothold of faith cannot withstand the doubt in their eyes, which usually sends me backsliding into the familiar emotional mud. If anything, my attempts to improve the situation seem only to deepen and complicate the distressful feelings among us.

On a day-to-day basis, my original family relationships are nowhere near as miserable as I generally conceptualize them to be. But there is a kind of dark current running through them that mysteriously holds me in thrall. It periodically erupts in painful and confusing confrontations that never yield to any kind of resolution. Over time, I increasingly choose to distance myself from them, and to live in terms of the more constructive bond I enjoy with my second sister, as well as the friendships that come into my life by following her example.

Now I am learning to accept that the pain of my first relationships is only there because of the corresponding love that refuses to die out from among us, even over decades of semi-estrangement. This is definitely healing my heart and restoring my appreciation of the value of the first three people in my life. The pain is one thing, and I am beginning to get an angle on that. But what about the confusion? Even when I have such an example of wisdom intimately guiding my life, and make sincere and earnest attempts to apply it to my problems, why am I so powerless in this primary sphere? Some crucial piece of the puzzle still seems to be missing.

Pondering the enigma of my own childhood, I continue to watch my young charges at play. Their fantasies are so irrepressible! One little boy likes to tie a beach towel over his shoulders and jump down into the sand from a park bench saying, 'Look, I'm Batman!' Phosphorescent wands simulating the weapons of Star Wars Jedi Knights are among their favorite toys. Items from our big box of costume clothing are in constant demand. Heroes and heroines are tremendously important to these young personalities, evoking powerful responses of love, adoration and imitation.

And not only heroes, but villains, too, serve as objects of enthusiastic infatuation. The same little boy who likes to be Batman frequently switches to being Darth Vader—same beach towel cape, same park bench, same jump. Toy replicas of the villainous Empire Robots are as cherished as those of the heroic R2D2 and C3PO. I notice that, especially for the very young children, it is far less important to be on the good (or bad) side of a story, than just to identify with any distinctive character. In fact, one thing that makes the children so endearing, even the most mischievous ones, is that in a very real sense they are creatures who have not yet tasted the fruit of the Tree of the Knowledge of Good and Evil. Their natural love is so alive and so unbounded as to ardently embrace the most violently opposing extremes with scarcely a hint of prejudice or preference. One rarely encounters such purely unconditional love in the world of adulthood. It teases my mind with the idea that perhaps unconditional love is in some sense predicated upon the childlike virtue of innocence...

Amidst my philosophical musings, it occurs to me to wonder if there could be some similarly innocent impulse of love behind my own childhood experience of periodically becoming the 'villain' in my family. Could it be that in my very early years, I in some sense assume or accept that role out of the same guileless innocence as the little boy with the beach towel pretending to be Darth Vader?

My family does not have television until I am nearly seven years old. My devout mother, bless her soul, never even tells us the usual fairy tales—only Bible stories, which always convey emphatic moral messages. But Bible stories also have heroes and villains. In fact, my parents' religious belief system depicts life itself as an ongoing struggle between the forces of Good and Evil. Could it be that in some pre-conscious moment I ingenuously offer to play the role of 'bad' when it seems to be wanted in our microcosmic family drama? And that in some primordial moment of semi-conscious communion, they understand me as agreeing to enact that saga with them?

If so, then perhaps the real source of estrangement between

myself and my original family is not my guilty hoard of unacceptable 'villainous' qualities, but simply my own opportunistic rejection of the villainous role as soon as I "learn" that the drama isn't "really" just a game! Indeed, confronted with the demise of my original willingness (in childhood's innocent spirit of non-preferential love and loyalty) to be their villain, there could be a sense in which they might subconsciously feel betrayed. Ironically, it may be my very rejection of the role of villain that actually awakens their distrust in me, rendering me more 'truly' villainous in their eyes! For in a sense, I am not merely rejecting a role, but opting out of the whole game, thereby becoming more of an outsider than their 'villain' ever could be. Perhaps herein lies the seed of the confusion that our painful confrontations are so blindly groping to disentangle...

Even as they whirl through my mind, I sense a germ of truth in these dizzying hypotheses. The clue to the enigma of my early childhood surely has something to do with the changes in perception, understanding, and presumption before, during, and after the advent of my personal ego—before, during and after my loss of childhood's original innocence. My mind is eager to grasp the full implications of these embryonic insights, but my heart leaps ahead, hearkening to the first faint tremors of a long-awaited release.

Truly there is a dungeon deep within the foundation walls of my self-defining citadel. My second sister's timely rescue obviously saves me from most of its frightful implications, but there is a part of me we have to leave behind— a part of me that chooses to honor the bond of love and loyalty between myself and the precious first three people in my life, even though it preserves a treacherous link to a life-long role I am prudently choosing not to play. There is a part of me that almost would sacrifice myself to their cause, a part of me that never quite forgets that the whole drama of Good and Evil *really is* just a game, a part of me that patiently stays behind, innocently true to the role of the villain, waiting in the dungeon. The long-awaited event my heart now senses is overtaking the moment as a powerful incoming tide of peace and reconciliation, dissolving at last those fortified battlements, allowing this long-forgotten cloister of my soul to be penetrated by tender afternoon sunbeams on the sandy shores of Lake Geneva.

How fondly the children begin to be caressed by my eyes, little bearers of treasure from the boundless seas of innocence, belonging, and being in the moment. At the ever-changing shoreline of inner and outer life, I see our endeavors, theirs and mine, carrying us past one another in symmetrically opposite directions. Their sandcastles of ego, full of heroes and villains and make-believe, are going up, up, up, joyously reaching for the sky of grown-up-alachia. Meanwhile mine are softly melting away, into the lapping lullaby of waves on the shores of the ocean of knowledge, as I aspire to the wisdom of saints and masters.

And yet, is there not a poignant likeness between my

procession and theirs—between my own compelling attraction to saints in general, and Guruji in particular, and the children's fantastical worship of larger-than-life heroes and villains? Are not their transitions into ego, as well as my transition out of it, being similarly mediated by powerful and vulnerable emotions of adoration and emulation toward individuals exemplifying the fuller stature to which we ardently aspire? As our brief sunny sojourn together is drawing to a close, I come to feel almost a mystical sense of kinship with the little folk at my feet.

Theoretically, we child-care helpers are expected to be with the children only during the morning and afternoon meetings of the adult retreat. But during the evenings when everyone meets together with Guruji for the usual chanting and dancing, some of my new little friends always come over to sing and dance with me. At night I share a cabin with one of the mothers and her two young daughters, while my husband is housed among the men enrolled in the full silence program. It almost seems as if the guardian spirits of Lake Geneva are conspiring to keep me in the world of childhood as much as possible during this time.

Then one afternoon near the end of the course, I am given the opportunity to take a break from childcare and attend an adult guided meditation session with Gurudev. As I approach the meditation hall, I find my husband standing outside the door, gazing up into the trees, holding a red carnation. I quietly walk to his side. We watch as Guruji opens the door of his cabin and walks toward us. My husband passes the carnation to me, and as Guruji approaches where we are standing, I hold the flower between my palms and offer it to him. He gently accepts it from my hands and proceeds to his seat in the front of the room.

I settle myself into a cushion next to my husband and near the door. Guruji leads us through a meditation which concentrates the energy in the seven central *chakras*, or energy centers, of the body. For nearly two hours, I sit as if transfixed upon a beam of power and light running up through my spine and out through the top of my head, until every cell in my body seems to be almost audibly humming with energy and bliss. I can barely feel my weight on the floor during the rest period at the end.

Realizing that my services are needed in childcare, I rouse myself in time to get back there before the parents come to find their children. As I quietly make my way to the door and step outside among the trees, my feet seem scarcely to touch the ground. It is like I am swimming in an ocean of joy that fills the space between earth and sky. I fantasize tumbling buoyantly in handsprings and somersaults all the way across the grounds, but restrict myself to hopping and skipping and twirling from tree to tree along the path. I could dance forever among the rays of sunlight streaming through the leaves, but compose myself to focus upon matching up pairs of little feet and shoes and socks and wrapping damp bathing suits in sandy towels.

As I am helping the last little girl, who can't remember where she is supposed to meet her mother, one of the course leaders approaches and begins to joke around with me. I especially like him because his corny manner of teasing reminds me of the silly things my father used to do to get me laughing when I was a little girl. In jest, my friend puts his arms around me from behind, with his hands over my mouth. He is pretending to chide me for breaking the silence by talking aloud to my young charge. Suddenly my tucked-away bliss breaks through, and before I realize what I am doing, I find myself crazily planting kisses all over the palms of my friend's two hands!

In the moment, I have become just like any little kid spilling over with excess of affection and energy. But this gentleman is no little kid, and neither am I. As I become aware of my actions, I suddenly feel extremely embarrassed and shocked at my own behavior. I break away and run to the bath house, splash cold water on my face, and shake myself in front of the mirror. What has come over me? I mean, it is one thing to immerse myself in the childlike virtues, but quite something else to find myself behaving like an unspoiled child in my full-grown body with a full-grown man who is not my husband! Dear God in Heaven, what if he were to misconstrue my intentions?

Fortunately, he is no longer there when I return to the little girl waiting for me outside. As I walk her to her mother's cabin, I fret over my misbehavior. What if Gurudev were to hear of this? Indian spiritual masters as a rule tend to be pretty conservative regarding behavior between the sexes. I suspect that Guruji might be more laid back than some, but still I would rather not have to be the person to test his boundaries. It irks me that I should have committed such a dopey misdemeanor.

This is the last evening of our retreat, and the children make a hit by handing out song sheets and leading the adults in a humorous bhajan reputedly composed by Guruji himself, celebrating the omnipresence of God in playful and childlike terms:

Om Om Hari Om (repeated 4 times to a lively melody)
"In the meow of the cat, in the chirp of the birds,
in the roar of the lion, I hear You."
Om Om Hari Om (4X)
"Underneath my roof, beneath the couch,
inside my closet, I catch You."

Om Om Hari Om (4X)

"Hiding in my cup, in the hem of my shirt,
in the sip of my coke, it's all You."

Om Om Hari Om (4X)

During their performance, five or six of the littlest singers crowd into my lap, including the little boy who likes to be Darth Vader, who keeps reaching for the microphone in my hand, unabashedly maneuvering to hog center stage. After our song, we present to Gurudev a patchwork quilt containing at least one fabric square painted by each child. The idea is for him to present it to the children of his charitable school in India. Guruji delights the children by putting their colorful masterpiece over his head and playing peek-a-boo with them for several minutes. I decide that a master capable of being such a child among children probably isn't going to get too upset even if he does find out about my embarrassing behavior of the day before.

The next morning, our entire group meets for a final hour with Gurudev in the meeting hall. The adults are out of silence now, sharing thoughts and reflections from their experiences of the past several days. I raise my hand and express to Guruji, briefly, how I began the week feeling apprehensive about my lack of experience with children, but now feel that the past few days have reunited me in profoundly meaningful ways with the world of childhood, including my own. Guruji responds to me with a penetrating look, as if assessing the progress of my soul.

A woman with a lot of health concerns requests his advice about her rather complicated situation. I watch him closely as he regards her with that same penetrating gaze and then speaks just one word: "Relax." His intonation is that of a mother caressing and soothing a frightened child. After a moment of silence, the woman begins to raise another question. Again, without ever diverting his gaze from her, Guruji repeats, in that same softly comforting voice, "Just relax." The woman becomes silent again for a moment, and then suddenly bursts into tears and laughter both at once. My own eyes become misty as I join the waves of gentle affectionate laughter that spread throughout the room.

Someone announces that the car is ready to take him to the airport, and Guruji energetically jumps up from his couch. He gathers an armful of the flowers that were given to him on his way into the hall, and begins to hand them out one by one to the devotees lining either side of the sidewalk as he makes his way to the curb. When he comes past where I am standing on tiptoe about two or three people away from the walk, he reaches over their heads with a grin and hands me a big red poppy. It gives me the feeling that he must be pleased, and perhaps amused, with whatever it is he sees through that penetrating gaze.

After Guruji's car disappears down the road, I find my husband and ask him if the silence program has been the same as the one we experienced together in California.

"A little bit different," he responds. "There is one technique we practiced several times, that I'm sure we never did in California."

Feeling a pang of envy over having missed out on a new technique, I further inquire, "Is there anything more you can tell me about it?" I know that masters often instruct their followers to maintain secrecy regarding the practices they have been taught. I don't want to intrude upon my husband's private spiritual life, but...

"Sure," comes his open response. "It involves the chanting or intoning of certain sounds that children make just before they begin to lose their innocence."

My heart bursts into laughter at the thought of the adults in the meditation hall chanting the sounds that children make as they are about to lose their innocence, while I amidst my duties with the children have been vision-questing into the mysteries surrounding my own loss and regaining of childhood's boundless innocence.

What is the use of envy, in a universe dancing with such playful mimicry?

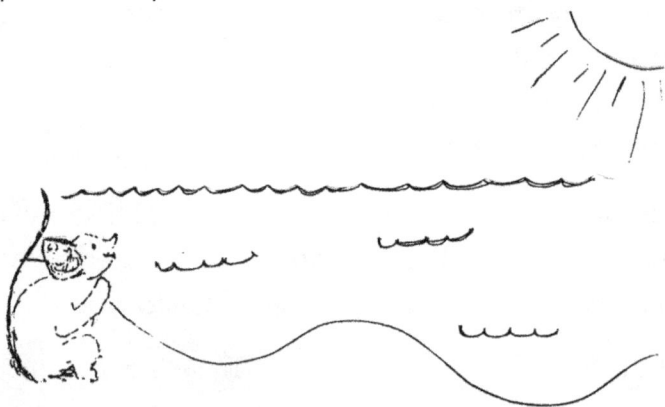

Ananda Mouse

Chapter Six

EGO EAST AND WEST

Basically, my morning ritual of listening to Guruji on audiotape is motivated by infatuation. I just want to begin my day by hearing his voice. Now, however, I find that the charm of infatuation is accompanied by another kind of urgency. So many shifts in perspective have occurred since my first encounter with him! I am beginning to feel slightly disoriented, as if my personal scheme of coordinates has gotten a bit scrambled. I need to try to understand the rules of this "inner game of Russian roulette" that I find myself so compulsively playing. I line up all my books and audiotapes in chronological order, and embark upon a systematic study of Sri Sri's discourses regarding the subject of ego in general, and ego dissolution in particular.

From my studies in the field of psychology, I am familiar with various theories and perspectives regarding the development and maintenance of ego, during childhood and beyond. The concept of ego dissolution tends, however, among Western psychologists, to be discussed almost exclusively in pathological terms. In fact, the theories I am familiar with consider ego dissolution to be virtually synonymous with insanity. A non-pathological version of the process seems scarcely to be dreamed of in our philosophies.

On the other hand, every Eastern master or saint that I know of emphasizes the importance of getting beyond the boundaries of ego. In spiritual circles devoted to the ideal of enlightenment, a great deal of focus seems always to be concentrated upon the delicate and elusive processes of "expanding," "transcending," "dissolving," "erasing," or even "crushing" the individual ego.

Sri Sri proves to be no exception to this trend. If anything, he carries the argument one step further than most. In his view, not only is ego dissolution prerequisite to spiritual advancement; even basic functional adult maturity requires liberation from the ego's constraining and retarding influence. It is a theme that figures prominently in his commentary upon the *Bhakti Sutras* (Aphorisms of Love):

Sri Sri: "What is enlightenment? To uncover is enlightenment. Uncover what? Your true identity, your true nature. And what is your true nature? Divine love. From every angle we come to this point that in all that we aspire in our life is full love, a Divine love, a love that is very ideal. So the purpose in life is to flower, bloom in that ideal love. Isn't it?

"Now, how to get there? How to have this? What obstructs us? This we have to see. What is really obstructing from being that innocent love is our ego. Now what is ego? Is it a substance? Is it something that exists?"

Aspirant: "It's real and abstract at the same time."

Sri Sri: "Yes. It's like a dream. A dream exists till it doesn't exist. You can't call dream real. You cannot call it unreal also, because you have had the experience, you saw. So, ego is simply being unnatural."

Aspirant: "If ego is so unnatural, why does every human being alive on the planet have an ego? Why did God do that?"

Sri Sri: "It is necessary. See, have you seen the seed? The seed has a covering on it. There is a shell, a membrane around the seed. You soak it in water, and it absorbs the water, and the seed grows bigger. And when the seed has sprouted, then the covering drops. Like that, ego is a necessary unnaturalness, which develops in you as you grow—when you are two, three years old. Before that, you are in that state of total, innocent, blissful love. Then this ego comes as a covering.

"Now all that knowledge does to you is to uncover this shell from you, make you again like a child, natural, simple, innocent. When you are natural, simple and innocent, there is no ego, understand this. Ego is not a substance. Like darkness is not a substance, it is lack of light. So there is nothing called an ego that is there as a substance. It is just lack of maturity. Ego is lack of maturity, lack of pure knowledge. That is what is ego.

"Now, how can this be overcome? Through understanding oneself, observing oneself, going deep into the self. So in the Bhakti Sutras, in the devotional aphorisms on love, it says: 'Knowledge is one of the aids to discover the naturalness.'

"See, it is half-knowledge that brings the ego. When knowledge is full, when it matures, ego drops. Simplicity dawns. One becomes very simple, natural. Then we say, 'Oh, the seed has sprouted; it has grown into a plant now.'

"So ego is just lack of total development, total understanding. That doesn't mean it shouldn't have been there from the very beginning. It has come. It has been necessary. But now you grow out of it.

"We see in the public, in society, people are aging, but mental age is getting standard or stagnant at certain particular time in life. Some are stuck in twenties. Some are stuck in thirties. Some are stuck in teenage. Their talk, their desires, everything goes only from that angle, from that level. There is not much awareness, awakening, openness.

"Knowledge is an aid to develop the innermost of you, which is love. In your innermost, you are love. Everyone is love. Everyone is made up of a substance called love. But why so much problem, is because of the shell that is ego, which is covering it like the seed is covered by the membrane. And this has to open up, leave space for the seed to sprout. For that we do some practices, some meditation, the Sudarshan Kriya. Going deep and uncovering, and removing the stresses and strains which wrap the love in you so tight, the love could not breathe or flower.

"Why someone does a mistake? Why did someone do some mistake, if they are full of love? It's just because of stresses and strain and tension and ignorance. This ignorance we call ego. This darkness—it's not a substance. When the light comes, it just vanishes. So the purpose of knowing, the purpose of every civilization, is to bring that Divine love, is to facilitate the opening of love..."

Gurudev does seem to be in agreement with Western thought on certain key points. For one thing, according to developmental psychology, it is at about the age of two or three years that we begin to grasp and explore the reality of being an individual among individuals. This is the age when we are developing muscular coordination and the corresponding faculty of will. Using these new abilities, we begin to construct ego as a functional sense of identity. We begin to delineate and identify who and what we are, and are not, in relation to others and the world around us.

Another point of correlation is the understanding that accumulated stress and tension tend to retard maturation. In psychological terms, stress and tension accumulate due to unresolved distress, or trauma, which becomes embedded in the physical and emotional system. We experience an unconscious or semi-conscious pull to go back and release our unresolved experiences, which distract us from appropriate forward growth and development. We inappropriately tend to identify with where we were at during our unresolved stressful moments; and thus ego (our sense of identity) becomes a form of ignorance—ignorance of who we really are, here and now. This is somewhat similar to Sri Sri's understanding of ego as ignorance, removable through practices that release and resolve deep-rooted stress from the system and thereby free us from the constraints of our limiting self-concepts.

But Sri Sri's reference point is not the Western concept of "age-appropriate behavior and identity." Sri Sri's reference point is "Divine love," a term not likely to be found in psychological literature. And "Divine love," as a reference point, leads to some greatly expanded insights regarding human maturation:

Sri Sri: "See, our capacity to love depends on how deep and open we can be. See, if it's a small pond, a small stone creates a big ripple in it. The capacity to love, if it's increased by knowledge, by depth, diving deep into oneself, capacity to love is also more. When the capacity to love is more, then your ability to know is more...

"We limit ourselves. We say, 'I belong to this culture, I am from East, I am from West, I am from Middle East, I am from Germany, I am from France, I am from this...' I become *something*. When I become something, my ability to love becomes limited. My ability to know becomes limited, through identification.

"Have you noticed the children? Have you noticed what is their talk, at ten-twelve years, between that age? They say,

'My dad is greater than your dad,' or 'My mom is better than your mom.' 'My teacher is better than yours.' 'My toy is better than your toy.' Have you seen them talking like this?

"I think most of the people are stuck at that age. They say the same thing when they grow older. Just the toys change. They say, 'My country is better than your country.' 'My culture is better than your culture.' 'My language is better than your language.' This is what is happening in the world. Do you see this madness in the world today? We think that things are great just because we belong to that thing. We are stuck in that limitation.

"Why not we shake up and see that all that exists in this world at this point, from time immemorial, all belongs to me. I am not just from America, just a German, or an Asian, or an Indian, or an African; but I am at home any- where, everywhere, with everybody. And all the wealth of humanity belongs to me, whether it is Gita or Koran or Bible or Sikhism or Jainism.

"All this wealth, a mature person would claim that whole thing as his wealth. See that? Maturity means someone who does not limit the wealth that is present in the world and divide it. He says, 'The whole entirety belongs to me, and I belong to everybody.' That is enlightenment.

"Ego is simply an illusion. Ego means separateness, that's all. 'You are different, I am different, I am somebody, I want to prove to you that I am right always, I am higher than you, I am bigger than you. Me and you, me and you.' That is the ego.

"And all this falsehood that we are building around us, the defenses we are holding around us, will simply fall off. On those ashes only this new phenomenon can dawn. As long as there is ego, there is no Divine love. And when there is Divine love, the ego—there is no sign of it. You can't track it down...

"See, the whole evolution of man is from being somebody. Being somebody is ego. 'Oh, I am great. I am very evolved. You are not evolved.' That is an ego. You see? Recognize that. From being somebody to being nobody, and from being nobody to being everybody: These are two steps in evolution.

"Even though one has attained the highest form of love, in the world they will live as a very simple, normal, natural human being. Because love flows when there is evenness...

"Love has a strange law—not like water which flows from high to low. Love flows in a plateau, where there is evenness... The Divine love flows when there is evenness, when there is connection. Divine love, even when it dawns for the person, the code of conduct for the person is to be very simple and natural.

"And this is what happens. Not, say, 'I am higher than you, I am bigger than you, I am holier than you, you are somewhere down below.' So-called people make you feel like a worm, that you are nobody, nothing. But one with a

Divine love elevates you, makes you 'You are like me, I am like you.' In evenness the love flows.

"To an enlightened person, everyone is form of God. Everyone is form of Divinity. An enlightened person, when he speaks, he doesn't speak from the position, 'Oh, you are all ignorant. I am very enlightened. I am going to tell you something.' No. He knows that the Divine has provided this beautiful knowledge, and It is taking back, coming in another form. It is just an exchange that is happening. In fact, it is all 'happening.' One observes, see, how this happens, how this happens, how this happens. That is being nobody.

"And from there, being everybody. Looking from the shoe of everyone. It's here that such a peace dawns in you that is unshakable. Nothing can rob you of this peace, and this joy."

Everyone

"Looking from the shoe of everyone" is another of Gurudev's phrases that brings to mind my second sister, whose manner of handling the family crisis around her pregnancy stands as one of the most powerful examples of unshakable peace and joy I have ever witnessed amidst the drama of everyday life. Guruji's words describe her truth so perfectly: Nothing could rob her of the joy that was flooding her soul in her first experience of motherhood. Even though it is somewhat embarrassing, I have to admit that by comparison, my own naïve contributions in support of her in that same situation seem conspicuously less mature.

Gurudev's timetable for maturity seems to have progressed pretty much on schedule in the case of my second sister. But for myself and most of the rest of my acquaintance, degrees of retardation appear indeed to be the norm, as Guruji so pointedly observes. Most of us still cling to our suffocating shells of ego long after their natural usefulness should have expired. Speaking for myself, I have to wonder, how exactly do I miss my developmental cues?

Under the auspices of Western insight-oriented psychology, I devote a fair amount of time and effort to self-study of my own ego-development. I come to understand that in my original family scenario, I occupy the classic position of 'scapegoat' in a 'dysfunctional co-dependent system,' and that I have been unconsciously struggling with this unwelcome identity all my life. I further come to view the estrangement between myself and my original family as a fundamentally healthy choice that I semi-consciously make in order to escape from the destructive consequences of my negative role-identity in an unhealthy drama. But in the process of rejecting my 'black sheep' identity, I become an over-achieving 'star student,'—another semi-dysfunctional identity in a variant of essentially the same co-dependent system. I formulate as my goal, to work toward a more healthy, functional relationship with the world around me—a relationship that is free of both the fear and negativity of my original identity, as well as the compulsiveness and over-compensation of its variant.

By Western standards, I can say that eventually I do succeed in accomplishing a more balanced ego-identity and emerge as a reasonably well-adjusted adult. But the unshakable peace and joy of Guruji's description, and my second sister's example, hold up a standard of maturity that I would have to classify as belonging to another league altogether. My 'well-adjusted adult' identity is perhaps preferable to its dysfunctional precursors, but it still is quite distinctly an ego identity; and I can feel the subtle feverishness of my disinclination to relinquish it.

So how is my sister able to breeze through her ego-stages so lightly, and drop them so naturally, in a world in which most of the rest of us cling to them so tenaciously and yet chronically struggle with their constraints?

Actually, the answer seems fairly obvious. My sister simply never takes any kind of negativity very seriously. Even identity itself carries very little weight with her. Considerations of name, fame, and reputation hold as little consequence in her mind as children's silly squabbles over who gets to go first. What she does take seriously is only the promptings of her own heart. She somehow never loses sight of the impulse of love which, as Guruji also points out, is always there at the core of every issue, every challenge, every overture.

My sister's genius for approaching life in this manner continues to this day to serve her admirably. Outwardly, she moves through the routines of a fairly typical middle-class American housewife, managing her household and her husband's family-related business, struggling with a challenging in-law situation, indulging her hobbies of painting and drawing in her little studio that occupies a sunny corner of the spare room over their garage, and showering her love upon her husband and their two daughters, both of whom appear to have inherited some measure of their mother's remarkable gift. They occasionally meditate, but otherwise maintain no formal ties with any church or spiritual tradition. Nevertheless, there is a graceful serenity pervading their home, which I always experience as exquisitely spiritual, in the deeply nurturing sense that unspoiled nature is spiritual. In fact, their home serves as something of a family Mecca. Every one of us takes exceptional delight in opportunities to vacation with them, and such visits are recreational for us in the truest sense of the word. We simply are drawn to our sister and her family as dear adorable beings with whom our hearts can dance.

In most of Western psychology, ego gets taken very

seriously as a fundamental psychological necessity that one cannot live sanely without. Worldly success and happiness are seen as critically linked to the kind of ego-identity we develop. Assuming that our egos have to serve us for a lifetime, it seems appropriate to go to great lengths to remedy their flaws and overcome their shortcomings. So, we embark upon arduous expeditions of introspection into their early childhood origins, and pursue elaborate therapeutic protocols for strengthening them and maintaining them in their optimally healthy and functional state.

In Gurudev's view, on the Eastern side, ego is an artificial structure serving a temporary purpose. It has a necessary protective function beginning from about age two or three and ending at some point not far beyond adolescence or perhaps early adulthood. It is described as a kind of dream or fantasy that the vulnerable young psyche enters into in order to develop the skills for negotiating the game of relativity that having a physical human body entails. We perceive the truth of the ego's make-believe nature as we first enter into it, but then we lose track of this larger perspective for several years, and eventually require some kind of external stimulus to shift our awareness back to the forgotten reality.

Guruji describes this process using the analogy of an actor in the theater: "You have all experienced this. Every one of us has experienced the Divine love. But we have completely forgotten it. We have no idea of who we are or where we are, what we have within us. That is why the Sutras. *Sutra* is to remind: 'come on, get back, it's in you.'

"It's like somebody working in a theatre, maybe Shakespeare drama, doing over and over for a few months, and then starts thinking they are that person, the shrew. She plays the role of Katherine and thinks that she is Katherine, herself. Now how can you tell her that 'there is no Katherine, you are somebody else'? Somebody acts as a Romeo and then starts thinking he is really Romeo. What will you do with him? You have to tell him, 'no, you have hypnotized yourself for acting that you are Romeo long enough.'"

Perhaps the naturally spiritual quality that is there in a woman's experience of pregnancy has something to do with my sister's ability to hold her own so well in the precarious situation she has to face at such an early moment in her life—barely past adolescence. Surely it is something deep and powerful in her experience that transforms her almost overnight from a carefree young art student into a fully blossomed woman, solidly grounded in the quiet certainty of her own strength and competence. Perhaps it is the stirring of new life in her womb that provides the necessary stimulus for the artificial scaffolding of childish ego to fall away and the Reality of Divine love to re-emerge in its mature forms of strength and centeredness, ecstasy and commitment.

I have no idea whether a spiritual master would perceive my sister as a fully, or only partially, awakened soul. My life-long love for her very possibly could be blinding me to limitations that she may still possess. In any case, the traditional commentaries suggest that most of us can expect the process of shedding our shells of ego to be somewhat arduous, to occur in stages over a period of time, and to require some form of assistance from a personal spiritual master or guide. In his Bhakti Sutra Commentary, Sri Sri outlines the process in simple terms:

"We don't love human beings," (i.e., when we are under the illusion of ego) "we love relationships. We love the wife or husband, boyfriend, girlfriend. Not because of what they are, not because they are wonderful human beings, but because 'they smiled at me, they cater to my needs.' So we love them. Our love is just very superficial. It is based on the needs.

"But if you'd stand up and take a look, the very same love develops into Divine love. The love that you have for objects and matter, for things and places and items, is not different from Divine love. It's not opposite to Divine love. Many religious people say: 'Oh, renounce the world, don't love the world, you can love God.' I tell you, the same love, transformed, becomes the Divine love. The same love comes out of its limitations, boundaries, conditions, and blossoms into Divine love.

"When there is love, there is no ego. Ego dissolves like the dewdrops with the sun. As soon as the sun comes, the dewdrops disappear. In the light of love, ego disappears."

In his next breath, however, Sri Sri is quick to point out that this isn't entirely an instinctive, unconscious, automatic process. There is a certain amount of pain involved; and some skill, some guidance, some conscious alertness is needed in order to handle the pain of ego dissolution in a manner that prevents the process from going awry:

"Why is that pain being experienced in love? Love and longing go hand in hand. If you long for something, then you love it. If you really love something, then you long for it. Isn't it? Can there be a love without longing? No. Longing is part of love, is the other face of love. That is why this is called as a couple. *Radha* means longing; *Krishna* means love. Krishna is the embodiment of love, and Radha is the longing. When you understand and be aware of this phenomenon, take this longing as part of love, then love becomes the Divine love, it grows.

"When we long for something, we don't allow the longing

to be there. We don't experience it, go through it. We want to put an end to it very quickly. We want to possess love. In the act of possessing, we destroy love. When you demand love, you are destroying love. It's like holding the flower from its petals. You are crushing the flower. And you are saying, 'I am holding the flower.' You want to hold the flower. But where are you holding the flower? Right at the blossom, and it gets crushed. And what you get in your hand is, your hand gets wet and it smells. That is what happens.

"Hold the flower where it has to be held. Longing or pain or hurt is part of love. Experience it. Be with it. Go through it. Then your love becomes so mature. There is pain in love because the pain is of the ego. The ego is disappearing and is being destroyed, crushed. And that crushing of the ego is painful. And there is no way out. Ego has to be crushed, in order to become a bigger, growing Divine love, who you are."

Guruji's advice about having to go through episodes of unavoidable pain on the path makes me slightly uneasy, especially since in some passages he also uses the words "intense" and "cruciating" to describe it, and invokes the symbolism of Christ hanging on the cross to illustrate his point. "Cross is the symbol of pain, and Christ is love. On the pain dawns love."

Dealing with pain is not one of my strong points, and I feel an impulse of rebellion gathering momentum in my gut in response to this teaching. From my Christian upbringing, I have absorbed the general assumption that since Christ has already gone through all the pain, His followers shouldn't necessarily have to live through any of it ourselves. Of course, there are the martyrs, but that is back in the dark ages. As a citizen of modern Western culture, I feel entitled to expect that by now someone must have invented some form of anesthetic to eliminate the necessity for almost any kind of pain. Also, the idea of love being connected to pain conjures up the specter of abusive relationships to my psychologically programmed mind.

On the other hand, I have to admit that sometimes I voluntarily choose to go through pain, and with beneficial results. During the hospital stay in connection with my miscarriage, I reject almost all pain medication in order to remain capable of practicing my meditation. Of course, I am totally anesthetized during surgery, which involves several hours of being cut open and taken apart and put back together. But even though the healing process afterward is accompanied by intense physical pain for several days, the doctors and nurses have to really persuade me to accept even a localized shot of darvan to ease and relax my system. Even then, after only two shots, I refuse any more. I value my mental and emotional clarity so much in this situation that I am actually choosing to accept a lot of pain as the price for maintaining it. I would never think of myself as a person who would exhibit such Spartan self-discipline, but in the exigency of the moment, it is the course I choose. And I definitely feel that I am able to make wiser choices at critical moments of this ordeal than I might were

I to allow my mind to become groggy with drugs.

In the realm of emotional pain, too, I am choosing to accept the pain involved in the love I share with my family, and find this to be marvelously healing to these relationships. If the pain that Guruji is prognosticating is just going to be basically more of this same sort of thing, perhaps it isn't anything to be getting up-in-arms about. Maybe it is more the prospect of pain, rather than the reality, that is pushing my buttons and stirring up resistance in my system.

But Gurudev's insistence upon the connection between pain and love does raise some questions in my mind. I am accustomed to regarding the phenomenon of pain-related love as one of the tell-tale signs of dysfunctional, and especially abusive, relationships—as in cases where battered women become self-destructively addicted to men who alternately abuse them and then beg for forgiveness, only to repeat the same cycle over and over. There are emotional versions of this problem which do not involve actual physical abuse; and it seems to me that there might be spiritual varieties of it to be avoided as well. I search my tape library with this question in mind, and soon realize that in answering people's real-life questions about problematic situations, Gurudev does make the distinction between healthy and co-dependent relationships, usually referring to the latter as "entanglements." And he does advise discretion in responding to dysfunctional emotional claims:

"Suppose somebody had fallen into a pit. You want to give

your hand, or give a rope to them. You are on the ground, and you give a rope to them; and they hold onto the rope, and they don't want to come. Rather, they pull you down; they pull the rope down. Then what will you do? Would you hold onto the rope and get down? You will have your foot first strong. Only if you are on the bank, can you ever pull someone onto the shore. Isn't it? And if their force is stronger than you, that is what is called entanglement. You get caught up. Whether it is in doing some service, or anything else. But if you get drowned, then neither will you be able to help them, nor will you be able to help yourself. Right?"

Quite clearly, it is one thing, in Gurudev's view, to be offering service in the 'I am here for you' spirit when one is solidly grounded and centered; and it is something else to have the motive to help, but lack the necessary strength and centeredness and find oneself getting caught up in the problem.

The difference between Sri Sri's discussion of these points, and their treatment in Western psychology, seems to be at least partly a matter of emphasis. Most Western psychological contributors are so heavily preoccupied with pathological situations as to scarcely notice the positive and centered varieties of selflessness that also are part of the human experience. And the idea that it may be appropriate to accept emotional pain as a healing and maturational aspect of healthy loving relationships is also rarely brought out, at least in material I am familiar with.

Sri Sri, on the other hand, elaborates upon the dynamics and the value of mature selfless service. He emphasizes the importance of accepting the painful emotions of longing and hurt that are part of even (and perhaps especially) the healthiest and most spiritual experiences of love. And he only seems to discuss the pathological type of thing when someone's question happens to bring it up.

A related area of uncertainty in my mind concerns the handling of ecstatic experiences, as for example, finding myself kissing that course leader's hands. I interpret this instance as an essentially positive impulse of childlike innocence and spontaneous affection. But it still disturbs me that I can shift so blithely into such socially inappropriate behavior.

Also, my mind seems to be flirting more and more with this fringey territory of ecstasy. Usually this involves singing. I have passionately fallen in love with several forms of devotional chanting, and often find myself singing aloud as I move through my daily routine. As long as I am at home, this is more or less acceptable. Other members of my household assure me that it doesn't disturb them; in fact, they say they rather enjoy it. But sometimes I suddenly realize that I am chanting aloud while walking down the sidewalk or pushing my cart down the aisle in the grocery store. So far, I always catch myself before anyone gets too wierded out; but no matter how earnestly I resolve to keep better control over my behavior, this tendency keeps taking me by surprise. In fact, the chanting seems to be going on in my head almost all the time; and I am often unaware of exactly when it starts coming out of my mouth as well.

Gurudev's commentary is only somewhat reassuring: "In the Kingdom of Heaven, there is a board hanging outside: 'Only Crazy People Allowed In.' In order to meet the Divine, you have to become crazy, go insane. It has a different mathematics, different passport, different norms. 'Be a Roman in Rome.' In that way, it has a different culture. And the culture and the qualifications and the passport is all about being crazy. Nobody has ever attained the Divine love without becoming crazy. You may not show it outside, but you have to be. So if someone tells you, 'you are crazy,' feel complimented. For a long, long time, I could not express my ecstasy, just knowing that people were likely to think it was crazy…

"When you have been in love with something, you always like to talk and talk and talk about it. It never tires you. Two hours, three hours, four hours, five hours—you don't even know how the time goes. Then people say, 'Oh, you are crazy about it.' Just a mild interest cannot evoke such amount of praise. That's why it is said you have to be crazy to praise so much. That is a sign of Divine love."

I have heard of people going through episodes of insanity on the path to enlightenment, although the only instances I am personally familiar with involve individuals with prior histories of schizophrenia or manic-depressive psychosis. This is probably not quite the same thing Guruji is talking about. In any case, I don't think I realistically need to be concerned about personally having to go through anything that Western psychology would define as psychosis.

But here Sri Sri is, once again, exploding the parameters of my psychological programming. Not only does he emphasize and elaborate upon non-pathological versions of ego dissolution, selflessness, and pain-related love; in these passages he is insisting upon a non-pathological version of insanity itself!

And his words describing it sound so familiar as I read them. In fact, by merely substituting the verbs "sing" or "chant" in place of "talk" or "praise," they offer a startlingly accurate description of my own emerging inner and outer reality. I have to conclude that quite possibly I am "going crazy" in Gurudev's "Kingdom of Heavenly" sense. If so, I only hope I can manage to stay within the ranks of those who "may not show it outside."

Eastern masters of my acquaintance tend to express rather critical opinions regarding Western psychology as a whole, and to particularly dispute some of the common methods and approaches of psychotherapy. I find this a bit odd, since it seems to me that Westerners who have undergone insight-oriented therapy, or who have studied the subject of psychology, are more likely to be open to the Eastern dimensions of wisdom than those who do not have the benefit of such exposure. Be this as it may, Gurudev's critique is as sharp as any I have encountered:

Aspirant: "Lots of people these days, in the process of healing their emotional bodies, are remembering childhood abuses—physical, emotional, and sexual. They are going through a lot of pain, and blame, and feelings of victim and persecution as a result. What would you do and say to help and guide these people?

Sri Sri: "One of the foolish things that the psychotherapists have been doing, is to establish the link of the event and the emotion strongly—stronger than what it was before. In spiritual practice we de-link the event from the emotions and the sensations. This is the first step you take. You feel a turmoil, an unpleasant sensation: de-link it from the happening of the past. Just observe that as sensation in the physical body.

"You have been given to believe that those events are there, imprinted in you permanently. So the more you try to clear it, the more it remains. And it goes on and on and on and on. People go day after day, month after month, year after year to the psychotherapists. And then you are made to believe strongly, all the pains are connected. And they take it back to the childhood days and put it there. It does not solve the problem in any way.

"It's like taking the garbage out of the garbage can and spreading it all over the floor. Now it is even everywhere. Ha, then you look into the garbage can: it is empty. But it is foul-smelling all over. This is what it has been doing. You are made to believe in the reality of the happening and carry it on as a permanent impression now also. And have self-pity. You feel more bad. 'Oh, I was abused'—more bad – 'I was abused'—more bad. And you keep feeling bad all along the path, all over the life. This is the most stupid thing that one could do.

"Your consciousness does not necessarily have just this past experience, few years. It has an infinite story. If you open up your consciousness, it has many many many many impressions—several lifetimes. Not only one, but also all that you have seen, that you have felt, even others' impressions are dumped in there. Why to stir all this? Burn them with the light of knowledge, with the light of awareness.

"You don't have to have self-pity on you. You have just experienced those events and experiences which were due to you. You completed those events. Only those which were due to you, you went through it and you finished it. That's gone. The whole past is gone. It's not more than like a nightmare, a dream. When a nightmare is over, you don't hang onto it when you wake up, do you?

"There is no need to interpret those things: 'Oh, this is why I had nightmare.' And then this interpretation of night-mare becomes even more strong in your mind. You are chewing it again and again and again. When you get a phlegm in your throat, spit it out. You don't have to chew the phlegm. This is what you are doing with all this. 'Oh! Phlegm! Phlegm!' I say, spit it out! It's all finished, gone. It's dirty.

"The very purpose of yoga is said to be *'Heyam duhkham anagatam.'* 'These particles of sadness or sorrow or problem which are ingrained in you—what do these meditations do?—they tear it apart, they release them, they completely dissolve them.' All the knots are un-knotted. The knots get opened up. Of the spiritual journey and practice it is said, *'Sat chit ananda.'* 'I am bliss consciousness.' I am not an abuse. I don't carry them. It doesn't stay there. I am just pure consciousness; this is what I am."

"Knowledge of Self heals you instantaneously, without you having to think about healing yourself. See what I am say-ing? Physical healing, of course, takes a little while. But if you don't handle the mind properly, the mental healing does not happen. People go to psychotherapy for fifteen, twenty years to heal some past wounds, old childhood wounds, some scars from childhood. It's not the way. With the knowledge of Self, the healing is almost instantaneous.

"There is a story about Mullah Nasrudin. His son came home from the school and said, 'Daddy, I got a prize in school!' Mullah asked, 'For what?' Son said, "They asked me

136   Ananda Mouse

a question. I answered the question, and they gave me a prize.' Mullah said, 'What question did they ask you?' Son: 'How many legs a cow has?' Mullah: 'What was the answer you gave?' Son: 'I said three.' Mullah said, 'What? You said three, and you got the prize?' Son said, 'Yes. Everybody else said two. I said three, so I got the prize.'

"That is what psychiatrists are. They know nothing about psyche, the mind, or consciousness. Simply drug the people. Make it complicated...

."I think it is mandatory for every psychologist to study Buddha. A psychologist can never be complete if he does not study Buddha. Buddha has given all the knowledge about the mind and its functions, in such a methodical manner.

You know, people go to psychotherapists who say, 'Oh, deep inside you there is sorrow, deep inside you there is something. Your mother has done something to you, your father did something to you.' This is such ignorance. I have known several people who had very good relationships with their parents; but after going to the psychologist, it all fell apart, because the psychologists attributed their misery to some childhood something, by just asking them questions.

"They do not know this simple thing, that every emotion has got a sensation in the physiology. Certain specific parts of the body resonate with different emotions. And when you observe the sensations, the emotions disappear and dissolve. And when you observe the sensations, you see that the body and consciousness are separate. And as you move on with the observation, you see you are simply linking the sensation with an event outside.

"Wisdom is, de-link the event from the emotion, and de-link the emotion from the sensation. Ignorance is, if you have some sensation, some sadness, some feeling, link it back again to the event. That makes you more miserable. And it sets the chain to go on and on and on. ...I mean, you may feel a little relief for a couple of days, because there is somebody there to talk to about all the problems. There is someone you pay to listen to you. There may be some value in psychology; I don't completely rule it out. There are some values. ...But I am saying, there are serious flaws.

"And it is high time that they recognize—I think that they are already doing it—the value of meditation, the value of silence. Unfortunately, none of the psychologists came in contact with a Buddha, or any enlightened one, any time in the past. They wrote volumes and volumes of books without knowing what is meditation, without ever encountering the depth, the source of the mind."

Gurudev's critical descriptions of psychotherapy do sound pretty familiar to me. One of the basic remedies in my mental health first aid kit is to think back from whatever is upsetting me, through recollections of similar previous experiences, until I arrive at my earliest memory of that same kind of feeling or situation. Then I use that early event as the basis for insight into the current manifestation of the problem. In theory, insights thus derived are supposed to lead to resolution of the problem in question; and to some extent, I feel that in my case they can be helpful in doing so. The process usually leads me to some kind of 'Aha' experience, which does seem to help me release distressful emotions.

But it is also quite true that over time this habitual approach has consolidated a self-image characterized by the mostly unhappy and discouraging experiences that I repeatedly relive through such regressive recollections. Even though I sincerely feel that I have benefited from using some of the methods of psychotherapy, I can also see Guruji's point, that my approach to psychological healing has probably been strengthening some of the same negative tendencies I am trying to overcome. Perhaps this may at least partly explain why progress through psychotherapy tends to be so painfully (and expensively) slow —a problem of which psychologists themselves are acutely aware.

I can see that Gurudev's approach to psychological healing has the advantage of coming from a deeper perspective than has generally been available to Western thinkers. The added dimension of transcendence obviously opens up an expanded range of methodology. In fact, my own reasons for becoming a meditation instructor, instead of a psychotherapist, reflect an intuitive conviction that the realm of transcendent experience offers a potentially superior approach to the resolution of psychological distress.

I tend to stop short, however, of seeing meditative practices as a substitute for traditional Western psychotherapy, and to promote them rather as helpful adjuncts, which can speed one's progress to recovery. But Sri Sri's protocols of observing and de-linking sensation, event, and emotion, and resorting to "knowledge of Self" seem to be rather emphatically presented as meditative procedures that could be used to actually replace the more tedious and self-contradictory Western methods. In his view, it would seem almost mandatory that psychotherapists be also, and perhaps even primarily, meditation instructors, equipped to offer guidance in a range of mental practices. This strikes me as a startlingly bold assertion.

I do recognize the processes of "observing" and

"de-linking" as experiences that often happen naturally during meditation. I am more accustomed to understanding them in terms of "restful alertness giving rise to spontaneous release of deep-rooted stress and tension." But nevertheless, I am certainly familiar with the restful alertness of meditation as a subjective experience of quietly "observing" and intentionally not engaging in (i.e., "de-linking" myself from) the more superficial thought activity—which I understand as part of the mind's normal way of releasing and dissolving stress. And in my own meditative practice, I often experience quite clearly that not only are body and consciousness separate, but also that there is something distinctly arbitrary about the way the mind hooks up emotion and event. Plus, of course, I am convinced beyond all doubt that regular meditation is profoundly beneficial to my own psychological and physical health. So why does Guruji's candid suggestion to employ meditative practices in lieu of Western psychotherapy suddenly sound so revolutionary to my mind's ear?

My memory flashes back to my junior year in college, Abnormal Psychology 181. The professor, one of my chief mentors of the era, is writing a formula on the blackboard:

$$Symptom = Stress/Ego\ strength$$

He explains that symptoms of psychopathology arise when the stress to the system becomes so great as to overpower the individual's capacity to maintain an autonomously viable ego construct for correlating inner, or subjective, experience with outer, or objective reality. In simple terms, an overwhelmed ego causes one to "lose touch with reality." Thus, he points out, there are three possible approaches to psychotherapy:

1. Treat the symptom. (Mostly done, in modern times through pharmaceutical intervention—sedatives, anti-depressants, psychotropic drugs, etc.)

2. Decrease stress. (Usually through lifestyle alterations: changing jobs, taking a vacation, etc.)

3. Increase ego strength. (One of the central aims of psychological counseling, but also possible through self-improvement endeavors such as yoga and meditation.)

My professor's favorable mention of meditation as a means of increasing ego-strength contributes to one of my strongest motivations for learning it. But Sri Sri clearly is *not* proposing the meditative processes of "observing" and "de-linking" for the purpose of increasing ego strength. On the contrary, in his view, these are procedures for dissolving the ego altogether, and establishing or centering one's conscious awareness in a completely transcendent basis of strength and autonomy!

To be sure, meditative practices can be said to accomplish all three of my professor's categories of psychotherapy: They do alleviate symptoms. They do decrease stress. And they do strengthen autonomy and centeredness (which to the Western psychologist is what our egos are supposed to be there for). Maharishi Mahesh Yogi, through whose organization I originally learned meditation, pursues the strategy of presenting Eastern techniques and knowledge in precisely these kinds of scientifically verifiable, bottom-line terms to our pragmatic and results-oriented Western mentality.

But Sri Sri has apparently decided that it is time for Western audiences to learn to understand and respect the wisdom of his tradition upon its own terms. His discourses on the subject of psychology contain an almost conspicuous lack of strategic accommodation to the Western theoretical framework. In fact, Guruji's discussions of ego, psychology, and meditation make it obvious that the meditative procedures he is recommending really do not fit anywhere in my professor's equation. Instead, he is proposing that Western psychologists adopt a therapeutic regimen whose candidly spiritual dimensions are almost outside the range of their discipline's theoretical comprehension. No wonder it sounds so revolutionary to my psychologically educated mind!

From the Eastern perspective of Gurudev's tradition, symptoms of psychological dysfunction involve more than just stress overwhelming ego strength. There is also the larger consideration of how distressful experiences come into our lives in the first place; and for this the laws of *karma* require to be taken into account. Sri Sri makes it quite clear that an important aspect of psychological healing involves understanding and accepting a kind of personal responsibility for our own misfortunes and distressful life-challenges: "You don't have to have self-pity on you. You have just experienced those events and experiences that were due to you. You completed those events. Only those which were due to you, you went through it and you finished it."

From the Eastern point of view, we certainly do not begin our lives with the mental and psychological "blank slate" hypothesized by some Western theorists. On the contrary, our minds come fully equipped with a complex array of impressions, based upon previous interactions, and mandating future transactional exchange. Guruji uses an analogy of stocks and loans to make the point:

"Good things happen to bad people and bad things happen to good people. This puzzles your mind. 'How come I have been so good - I never did wrong to anybody - and why this wrong thing is happening to me? And this gentleman does such a horrible thing and he seems to be enjoying.' This is very funny. This is very strange.

"No, I tell you, even in the good man, deep inside, hidden somewhere, there are impressions. They come up, and one has to face the consequences. Even in the so-called bad man, there are deep impressions in him which bring out some nice things in their life, too. So there are different piles within each individual. A lot of stock you have. Loans somewhere, and you have loaned elsewhere. So where you have loans, there you have to repay. And where you have loaned, you will get back. You know? That will be credited to you.

"So it's both. In one hand you are receiving. In another hand, you are giving elsewhere. This give and take is happening inside you. That's why it appears to be very complicated. It seems to be injustice sometimes. 'Oh, I have been so good, never did any wrong, but why this wrong thing is happening to me or to my people?'"

Furthermore, according to Guruji, every item in our complicated piles of impressions is there on account of our own intention:

Sri Sri: "Your karma is not on your action, but your intention. If you look at someone, and there is a jealousy feeling stirring inside you, and you act out of jealousy; then you are making that karma. But when you are acting without having any sore feelings or tightness in you, just very natural, then that is their karma. Do you see? The mechanism is very delicate and very intricate. You have to go really deep into it. Whatever I have said, each sentence, you have to really peep through it. Otherwise you will not understand this. It's very delicate…

"Karma is what? Simply understand this, to put it in very simple words: the impressions made on your mind by your intentions. Period. Very simple. All the impressions which associate with the feelings which get into your consciousness."

Aspirant: "It seems to imply some attachment to the

action that is going on."

Sri Sri: "Yes. Intention means that attachment is there to the action, immediately."

Aspirant: "So animals don't incur karma?"

Sri Sri: "If they are doing something which is associated with a feeling and with an intention, yes, they do, sometimes. But their ability to do that is very limited."

Aspirant: "So then it is true that we do not hurt another, but we merely deliver karma. But we can create karma for ourselves."

Sri Sri: "Yes, yes, yes."

Aspirant: "And that's the basis for forgiveness."

Sri Sri: "Yes. Lack of awareness multiplies the karma. It repeats. Lack of awareness means what? Simply repetition of what is there already. So there is already tension, violence; and that repeats. And that goes on and it repeats, repeats, goes on in the cycle.

"How did it get there the first time? It got there with an impression. How did it get in there? An impression cannot come into you in your sleep. When one is aware, an impression gets in. See, it's like a habit. You develop smoking habit. Once it becomes a habit, it gets into your unawareness. It becomes a product of your unawareness. Then you go on smoking. You are not aware of it, even."

In Gurudev's analysis, the psychological problem lies not in the tendency for impressions, or stress, to overwhelm ego strength, but in the factors of intention and attachment through which our impressions bind, define, and limit us to the narrow, weak and artificial constructs of ego identification. The road to mature psychological health and well-being does not involve probing into the past and going into all the details, because such procedures mostly just reinforce our intentions and attachments and thereby deepen our impressions. Instead, the road to mature psychological strength involves strategies to reposition our conscious awareness in ways that weaken the bonds of intention and attachment, and anchor our sense of self in the unlimited, unconstructed domain of transcendence, i.e., through devotion, acceptance, meditation, and surrender:

"Devotion has the power to burn down any karma. Instead of digging into the past, look at it, whatever is right now, and merge, go further. Meditate. Go deep into it. Do some practice. You can burn down all those karmas. It's very much possible. Karma is just the impression that the mind has carried deep inside. So those impressions attract those events around. But by surrender, by meditating, you can erase all those impressions to a great extent. To a very great extent, those could be erased."

From Guruji's perspective, true healing necessarily draws upon the resources of the soul. It reminds me of many accounts I have read of individuals who experienced spontaneous remissions of cancer and AIDS. The quest for healing, as well as the sharing of such experiences with others, frequently draws us into sacred space, opening our hearts and flooding our awareness with deeply felt emotion and inspiration. Devotion, acceptance, surrender, meditation: Such approaches may not lend themselves readily to scientific research, but their power is seldom questioned by those whose lives have been blessed with healing even after science and technology pronounced them incurable.

Gurudev's description also reminds me of the practices of repentance and forgiveness that are strongly emphasized in my early religious training. In a scenario where intention and attachment are the key factors attracting distress into our lives, these profoundly surrendered and relinquishing virtues would obviously play a critical role in healing at all levels. It suggests a fascinating insight into the way Christ's miracles of healing, as described in the Bible, are often preceded by some affirmation of Divine forgiveness:

"Thy sins be forgiven thee…
Arise, take up thy bed, and go unto thine house."

Matthew 9: 5,6

It is apparent that Sri Sri's larger perspective on psychological healing not only reflects the added dimension of transcendence; it also draws upon a vastly expanded time frame. In the Eastern view, impressions in the human psyche have their roots not in early childhood, but in virtually unfathomable antiquity, hearkening back through countless lifetimes. A famous quote from one of the earlier masters of Sri Sri's Shankaracharya tradition claims that we live through some four hundred million lifetimes before attaining a human birth. Guruji himself refers to the many classic issues, or *samskaras*, around eating, sleeping, and sex as representing our "oldest impressions," because, "for sure, in all of our previous lives, as a dog, as a cow, as a monkey—in all these animal lives we have been doing them over and over again."

Against such a panoramic backdrop, the very idea of trying to establish definitive causal relationships between present day problems and specific events that have happened only a few decades ago, seems rather pointless. If we accept the premise that human consciousness represents a multi-millenial accumulation of previous life experience, then interpretations restricted to events of this lifetime become arbitrarily abstracted from most of their relevant context. Such narrow interpretations would logically possess very limited power to resolve problems involving deeply primordial impressions. Perhaps, once again, this helps to explain why chronic disorders of eating, sleeping, and sex have tended to be particularly resistant to the approaches of Western psychotherapy.

Of course, I realize that the guiding lights of Western psychology might not be quite ready to adopt the previous-life premises of Eastern thought. For me, however, the notion that we come into this world with a wealth of past-life history has established itself as nearly self-evident reality. I have a long-standing interest in the subject, awakened by a short series of cathartic personal experiences with past-life recollection. I am also familiar with several well-documented case studies involving the ability of human memory to access previous-life material. Most of the case studies involve hypnotherapeutic regression, a process with which I have no personal experience. But the contents of the subjects' recollections certainly ring true to my favorably predisposed mind.

My own past life experiences arise spontaneously during the healing crisis precipitated by my miscarriage and subsequent surgery. At first I try to question whether these startling recollections really could be what they seem to be. But over time, my mind grows weary of maintaining the contrived logic around other possible interpretations, and ultimately I conclude that I simply cannot argue with my own irrecantible memories.

The experience of remembering certain past-life incidents leads me to far deeper spiritual and psychological resolutions than I have been able to achieve without their input. There are several human beings on this planet whom I might never be able to forgive for their seemingly arbitrary and malicious maltreatment of myself and others, were it not for the realization that our semi-conscious histories have been heart-rendingly intermingled in other places and times. Also, my personal recollections of living as a member of the opposite gender in a dark-skinned race have strengthened my ability to empathize with people who are racially different from me now. My gut feeling is that if more people were to realize that they could easily find themselves wearing the skins of the oppressed next time around, many long-standing social inequities might quickly be resolved.

My references to personal heritage, too, have been expanded by the experience of past-life recollections. Knowing that I represent a far more complex ancestry than the purely genetic one familiar to Western thought, has enhanced my interest in other cultures and religions, and awakened a sense of kinship connecting me to several divergent traditions. I experience a particularly strong and heartfelt affirmation when Gurudev makes his point that a mature person would claim all the cultural and spiritual wealth of the world as his or her own heritage. To me it seems quite likely that every living member of today's human family may have literally contributed to several different branches of civilization at various pre-memorial times; and we eminently deserve to claim all of this priceless legacy as our own rightful inheritance.

Guruji certainly seems to feel very little reticence about challenging Western preconceptions of reality. My Western mind kind of cringes, for example, over his statement that psychological healing is "almost spontaneous, with the knowledge of the Self." To my scientifically-trained intellect, this sounds like such an outrageous claim. It seems almost inconceivable that a modality of healing could claim to produce "almost spontaneous" results, in any sober and honest sense of the term. True, I understand that the phrase "knowledge of the Self" refers to that deep experiential certainty of one's own expanded reality, which is characteristic of meditative transcendence. And I suspect that Guruji's definition of the term probably also means to include something of the wisdom of how to handle the mind, which he so often emphasizes. Certainly knowledge of transcendence and Gurudev's wisdom do rank among my most valued personal resources. But can I seriously credit them with powers of "almost spontaneous" psychological healing?

My mind wanders through my own brief experience—less than two years—with Sri Sri's "knowledge of the Self." Indeed it is true that gentle waves of healing and reconciliation are flowing through my life, subtly transforming almost every dimension thereof. I feel more deeply at peace and at one with myself, my spouse, my family, my world, than I can recall from previous experience of any age in any life. And somehow this is all happening with very little flash or fanfare. In fact, I really have no idea how or why it is happening to me at all. All I am doing is following my heart, and you could hardly even call that "doing." It is something that is just happening—"almost spontaneously" would be, in fact, the perfect description! And in this process, I also suspect I am being "healed" of potential ailments and distresses that I may never know I would have had. It all looks kind of mysterious to my mind—but its results in my life are indisputably real, and deeply gratifying.

As I contemplate my various experiences with both Western and Eastern approaches to psychological healing, it strikes me that although, from a Western point of view, the two systems are based upon seemingly irreconcilable premises; from the Eastern perspective their discrepancies do not seem difficult to resolve.

To Western psychology, individuation is the name of the game; and ego is the all-important 'reality principle' by which we recognize, understand, and maintain appropriate boundaries between inner and outer, self and other.

To the Eastern masters, individuation is only a game; and even though we temporarily need the artificial construct of ego in order to learn to play that game, in maturity we drop our ego-identities as we return to our original un-deluded knowledge that boundaries are illusions. There is no inner and outer. There is no self and other. There is only an indescribable, seamlessly whole, all-encompassing Reality, which is, in fact, our very own truth. Guruji calls it "Divine love," which "is not an emotion, it is our very existence."

In the Eastern interpretation, it is true that, for practical purposes of maintaining and participating in the illusion of manifest creation, we do continue even in full maturity to go along with the game—to chop the wood and carry the water, as the saying goes. But we go about our daily activities within the fully established awareness of our unbounded Reality motivating, guiding, and indeed actually doing every action—more like things are "happening through" us, than as if we as individuals are "doing" things. And although we play the game of self and other, it is with such fully mutual compassion and empathy that even competition and conflict seem to exist only for fun. In Gurudev's view of maturity, we anchor our centeredness not in some adult-level "viable ego construct," but in the innocent, unconstructed depths of "unshakable peace and joy," which we access more and more fully through the opening of the heart.

To the educated Western mind, Eastern thought seems frustratingly addicted to unverifiable and scientifically doubtful spiritual and subjective material. But to the no-mind of an Eastern master like Gurudev, the Western perspective seems frustratingly stuck in an immature commitment to ego-related boundaries—self vs. other, subjective vs. objective, secular vs. sacred. As our material-istically programmed Western minds laboriously expand to accommodate the increasingly unbounded concepts of 'cutting edge' science, technology, and cross-cultural exploration, we invent 'new age' terminology to describe our 'breakthrough' discoveries: "paradigm shift," "Gaia," "hundredth monkey effect," etc. But to the realized Eastern sage, all this probably looks like nothing more than typi-cal, if somewhat overdue, post-adolescent growing pains. From the perspective of enlightened maturity, it would appear that the ego-oriented Western mentality shrinks down to little more than a section of detail that has lost self-awareness of its orientation to the larger whole; and even that may be viewed as just a natural temporary episode of the human maturation process.

Regardless of whether I choose to call it 'paradigm shift' or 'growing pains,' I am certainly learning to appreciate that the assimilation of new understandings into my existing worldview is a complex process occurring in stages over time. I have been living with an awareness of at least certain episodes of my own past-life history for several years, and for fully two decades have been exposing myself to meditative transcendence. Even so, Guruji's commentary makes it obvious that I am only beginning to explore the full implications of these larger dimensions of experience.

As I ponder Gurudev's critique of Western psychology, glimpses of the vast potential for healing and growth through the transcendent and subjective technologies of the oriental hemisphere begin to pierce like rays of sunlight through the widening cracks and crevices in my materially encoded mind. How laughable we must seem to the masters of the East as they observe our smugly self-important "experts" trying to employ their elegant and powerful mental technologies as "adjuncts" to our crude and barely functional therapeutic modalities. And what keen sensitivity, tenderness, and patience are there in Guruji's words, which never become too unkindly sarcastic even while sharply and clearly conveying the remonstrations that are needed for (hopefully) shaking listeners like me out of stagnation, and into healthy maturity.

As I research this subject, Guruji's playfully spontaneous yet masterful expressions soar through my mind like deftly aimed arrows of unflinching love, repeatedly piercing to the quick through my occidental armors of individuation and ego identification. Taken one by one, their stings seem relatively minor—just enough to alert and realign me a few degrees this way or that. But as my quest progresses, their collective impact crescendos, overtaking me in an onslaught of wisdom and understanding before which my mind, my heart, my soul can only bow down in awed and chastened surrender.

So it is, once again, that Gurudev's sagacious love is drawing me into the posture of surrender. How many times, and from how many angles, has the mystery of surrender overtaken me, each instance flavored by its own unique subtleties of ecstasy! In savoring the moment of this one, I sense the existence of some kind of deep connection between ecstasy itself and the dissolution of ego. Perhaps the pilgrim's progress to ego dissolution gradually becomes complete as more and deeper ecstasies of love and surrender are tasted to the full...

Or perhaps ecstasy and the dissolving of ego are simply one and the same.

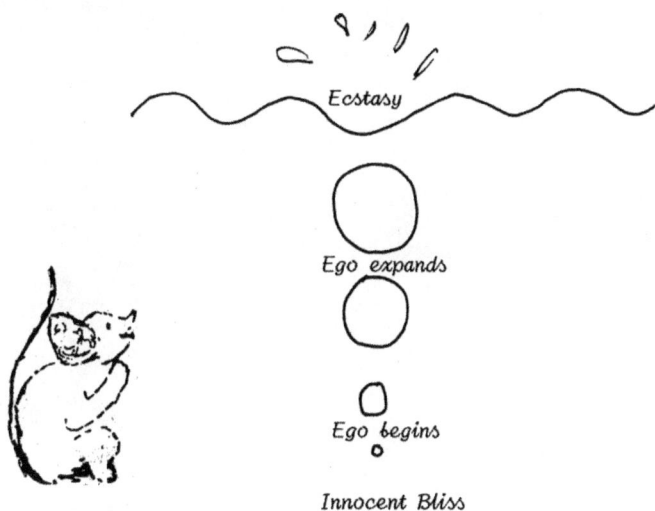

Ecstasy

Ego expands

Ego begins

Innocent Bliss

Chapter Seven

THE SACRED WATERS
ARE HOLLOW AND EMPTY

My enquiry into Sri Sri's discourses upon ego does succeed, to some extent, in resolving the questions of my mind; but the deeper queries of my heart are only becoming more urgent. Her bravest wish has come true: there is no denying that I am in the grip of a powerful personal connection with an exceptional being. But in what way, and to what extent (if any) are my attraction and my feelings actually reciprocated by him? What sort of behavior, or what angle of orientation, is really appropriate for relating to him? No doubt, this is an essentially spiritual liaison; but how is one's spiritual relationship with an embodied master supposed to be different from, or similar to, one's relationship with God? And to what extent can my blissed-out crazy mind even be trusted, either to guide my behavior, or to negotiate the unfamiliar terrain upon which my heart so incautiously presumes to tread?

No amount of analysis and understanding seems adequate to assuage the growing restlessness in my soul. Guruji is still in North America. His tour proceeds from Lake Geneva to the West Coast, and concludes with a retreat in Santa Fe. I do not expect to attend any more of this; but just prior to the week in Santa Fe, someone offers me a partial scholarship on the basis of my services in childcare at Lake Geneva.

My heart leaps at the opportunity. Never mind that it entails a three-day drive in my hundred-fifty-thousand-mile-old vehicle, or that my husband (with his reassuring genius for keeping anything on four wheels miraculously moving) cannot accompany me due to occupational commitments. Anyway, I'm not traveling alone. An intrepid girlfriend with a similar husband situation wants to collaborate on the trip. I know that she has, if anything, even less competence with unpredictable vehicles than I do. But to my exuberant heart, the prospect of her company extends an aura of credibility to the venture. Within twenty-four hours, we are packed and on our way.

Our drive is peaceful and scenic. My companion, happily, shares my contemplative aloofness with respect to mainstream media; and we cover the miles in friendly silence, occasionally punctuated by light conversation. We choose a two-lane route through the sparsely populated and breath-takingly beautiful desert highlands of northeastern New Mexico, where some of the winding roads become so steep that pedal-to-the-metal chugs us forward at no more than twenty miles per hour. On several occasions, the apparently cloudless blue skies suddenly produce brief but wild thunderstorms which vanish as abruptly as they appear, restoring us to peaceful terraces of sunshine, cedar, and sagebrush that seem to harbor scarcely a memory of precipitation in any form. I sense the presence of an untamed and unrelenting soul within the becalmed expanses of desert wilderness, which lures me into fantasies of having embarked upon some timeless, enchanted odyssey.

For the last leg of our journey, we reluctantly return to the interstate highway approaching Santa Fe. Then just as we enter the outskirts of the city, my car's engine stops. As we coast onto the shoulder of the road, I notice that the heat gauge has climbed to the top of the red line above "hot," and all the warning signs on the dash are lit up. I pop the hood and pull out the dipstick: Its tip is as dry as the sun-baked asphalt beneath my feet.

My car burns oil, at the rate of about half a quart to a tank of gas. At my husband's insistence, I am carrying a whole case of the appropriate brand, heeding his solemn warning that if I ever let the reservoir become completely empty, it's the end of the engine. But I still have half a tank of gas, and have been conscientiously adding oil with every fill-up. Evidently my car's rate of oil consumption has suddenly accelerated. In panic, I open the hatch-back, pull out a quart of oil, and empty it into the engine. Still no reading on the dipstick. It takes three and a half quarts to bring the reading up to full. Three and a half quarts is a complete oil change.

One of my worst nightmares has apparently come true: I am stranded on a highway in a strange city with a seriously disabled vehicle and no emergency funds. Contemplating my own foolhardiness, I sit behind the wheel, explain our plight to my companion, and wait for the next highway patrolman to notice us. I have no idea what I am going to do. My husband is working on an outdoor construction site a thousand miles away and unreachable by phone. My companion's personal resources are even slimmer than mine. Her nervous laughter is still friendly, but not particularly reassuring. I suppose I will have to contact the Santa Fe organizers, in the hope that someone among them can help us out of our predicament. I do not look forward to introducing a financially challenging emergency into their no doubt already hectic last-minute preparations.

There certainly don't seem to be many patrol cars on Interstate 25 today. We sit parked by the side of the road, emergency lights flashing, for nearly half an hour. The midday sun is becoming quite uncomfortably hot. Impatiently, I turn the key in the ignition to see if at least the fan might still work. The engine starts to sputter! I give it some gas, and it turns over almost as smoothly as if nothing has ever gone wrong—no warning lights, heat gauge hovering within normal range.

Scarcely daring to believe in my sudden reversal of fortune, I shift into gear and start rolling forward—second gear, third gear, fourth, and fifth, as once again we merge with mainstream traffic. I drive nervously, monitoring the heat and oil indicators every few seconds, but neither registers any further aberration. We arrive at our destination with time to spare. I once again pull out the dipstick and learn that the oil consumption during our final two hours of driving has been no greater than my car's previous norm.

In relating our near-misadventure to the gentleman standing in line ahead of us at the registration table, I learn that some cars can burn a lot of oil quickly driving in the high altitudes where we have been. But for an engine to start back up like that, after losing all its oil and overheating and dying, does seem pretty amazing—maybe not quite a miracle, but certainly very lucky! It gives me a sense of being taken care of—though I also decide we will take an indirect, southerly route home to avoid further high-altitude touring!

Upon completing our paperwork, my companion and I settle ourselves into our assigned room, which we share with two other women. Our accommodations are located in a once-elegant motel that forms part of an expansive, but currently unoccupied, resort facility, not far outside Santa Fe. Leaving my roommates to gossip and/or meditate, I set out alone to stretch my limbs by exploring the grounds.

The place is a study in incongruity. Within its boundaries, the muted desert pastels have been somewhat garishly imposed upon by the introduction of flowering shrubs, bright green grasses, leafy trees, and a pond, still stocked with a few colorful breeds of fish. Apparently the intention has been to create a tropical atmosphere. Much of this ambitious landscape artistry is awkwardly expiring beneath the peacefully persistent erasers of sand and sagebrush. But the central terraced gardens between the main building and the pond continue to hold their own in a kind of derelict luxury, as if not yet quite awakened from languid dreams of a glamorous youth. They charm me in a manner reminiscent of childhood explorations around old abandoned homesteads.

I follow a path from the garden through an untended area of tall straw-like grasses and weeds, out to the large cracked concrete basin of an Olympic-size swimming pool. The parched tangle of grass and thistle sprouting through crevices in the cement now supports a lively population of grasshoppers, diving and soaring as if in mimicry of bygone swimmers. I marvel at their revelry in the heat of a glaring sun, which is rapidly dehydrating me.

Scanning the environs for a source of liquid refreshment, I

notice a wooden concession stand whose peeling pink sign promises fresh fruit and vegetable juices, along with an assortment of health food snacks. Its service windows are boarded up, and circumambulation of its perimeter fails to manifest even so much as a coin-operated pop machine.

Heading back across the sand towards the main building, where drinking water, at least, is sure to be available, I come upon another wood-framed structure, whose signboard offers varieties of massage and bodywork. Thirst notwithstanding, I opt for one more investigation, thinking that I might find a left-over massage table suitable for trading hands-on with fellow retreat participants. After three days on the road, I could certainly appreciate some relaxing touch therapy.

As if to encourage my fantasy, this building is less securely protected against trespass; and I soon find a door that pushes open easily. A quick survey of the interior, however, reveals that it has been converted into a storage shed for gardening paraphernalia. Stone and terra-cotta pots, planters and urns litter the floor of the main room in disarray, suggesting the contours of a ghostly banquet table whose erstwhile succulent diners have abandoned their roots amid the dregs of potting soil. Side rooms contain a dusty assortment of long-handled implements, coiled watering hose, etc., none of which bear any resemblance to the coveted massage table.

The nearest entry into the main building leads through a hallway with a wall displaying a collection of frameless old mirrors in a variety of sizes and shapes, having been extracted from items of Victorian and provincial furniture. The mirrors look uncomfortably naked, their chipped and jagged edges giving the lie of exposure to elegant beveled contours. Perhaps in this they reflect the embarrassed spirit of an establishment whose hospitality, though still comfortable, falls conspicuously short of maintaining the full attire of its pretentious self-image. Offering an homage of compassion to my tattered ghostly host, I bow before the fountain at the end of the hall and gratefully quench my thirst.

Just beyond the fountain, another wide corridor intersects with the hall of mirrors; and I notice a row of shoes along its wall. The trail of footwear leads to a set of double doors opening into a large room, which I infer to be our meeting hall. A pleasant din of activity greets my ears as I approach the entry, but subsides as I turn around and make a detour out to my car in the parking lot. My excuse is the need to bring in an armload of cushions and back support, but I also want a moment to shift my orientation. Meeting people is different than meeting places.

Returning with more sociable intentions, I step out of my sandals and confront the faded glory of our meeting room, which features dark marble floor tiles and an entire wall of windows overlooking an empty stone patio with stairs descending into a neglected section of the garden. I arrange my cushions and backjack so as to minimize bodily contact with the hard floor, and circulate to exchange amenities with acquaintances from previous retreats.

One of them is the teasing friend whose hands I kissed at Lake Geneva. He greets me cordially, and insists that I accompany him upstairs to the hallway outside Guruji's room. It seems that Guruji himself has just arrived, though only a few people are as yet aware of this. I feel a little awkward at being suddenly included among what I imagine to be a select inner circle around the master, and repeatedly ask my friend if he is sure it is really appropriate for me to be standing there, right outside Gurudev's door, just after his arrival.

Very shortly, the door opens, and there is Guruji himself, greeting us warmly, accepting flowers from those who offer them, and nodding a personal recognition to nearly every individual, myself included. Thrilled and excited to find myself once again in the magic of his presence, I follow along as the local organizers lead him on a brief but leisurely tour of the grounds, pointing out where the meals are to be served, where the introductory course is to meet, etc. As the afternoon sun extends its long golden rays in lazy slopes from the west, Guruji returns to his room for private conferences with the course leaders, inviting the rest of us to have dinner before joining him for evening Satsang in the hall. Disliking the long lines which usually materialize at the beginning of course buffets, I return to my room and indulge in a late afternoon meditation, which charms me into such timelessness that I nearly miss the meal altogether.

I dine hastily and proceed to the hall. Most of my fellow course participants are already seated and chanting merrily to chase away the sleepy ghosts of disuse from the shadowy rafters of the great high-ceilinged ballroom whose marble floor is now almost invisible beneath colorful haphazard rows of cushions and blankets. The set-up is typical: At front and center a raised platform features Gurudev's seat, draped in silk and flanked by large potted ferns. To the right of the platform sit the musicians with their instruments and sound equipment. The video camera perches prominently upon its tripod just forward of the middle of the room; and the black umbrella stage lights (to be turned on when Guruji begins his evening discourse) tower over everything like slender sentinels right and left. Stepping carefully between back-jacks, I settle into my cushy little nest and close my eyes to focus upon the chant in progress.

As the music gains momentum, Guruji enters the hall, singing aloud and raising his hands—like a classic

"Laughing Buddha," only without the big belly. Rising to my feet in honor of his entrance, I want to laugh myself. There is something heartwarmingly humorous about a bearded, long-haired, white-robed master being obviously in a party mood. Accepting handfuls of flowers while walking toward his chair, he nods to the musicians, who obligingly step up the tempo: *"Jaya Jaya Shiva Shambo, Jaya Jaya Shiva Shambo..."* The urge to move becomes irresistible, and I join the swelling chorus of dancers at the back of the room as the drummers ascend to hog heaven. Fortunately our lead singer, a jazz professional with a powerful voice, is able to impose enough musical discipline to prevent our enthusiastic self-expression from degenerating into mere rambunctious noise-making.

As we sing and dance, Guruji closes his eyes and enters a meditative state. It is a familiar scenario: we continue singing chant after chant until he opens his eyes and gestures for the microphone. There is an intimate and comforting mutuality about the arrangement, as if his silence is fueling our devotional energy, which in turn is deepening his transcendence. Like many Eastern masters, Guruji is reputed to take very little sleep, preferring to sustain himself through brief episodes, like this one, of silent, inward *samadhi*. It awes me that he would so innocently confide his personal need for rest to our company; and yet it also lends a homey and relaxed air to our evenings with him.

As he opens his eyes and pulls the microphone forward, our music subsides and an absorbing, expectant silence prevails for several minutes. The video camera operator stealthily moves into position and signals for the stage lights to be switched on. Smilingly, Gurudev closes his eyes again —partly, no doubt, in response to the bright lights, but also as an invitation to us to savor the beauty of the moment. I close my own eyes and gratefully allow the still-ness to fill my soul.

It seems I blank out for some time, for I suddenly become aware that Gurudev is coming to the end of a gentle dis-course:

"You will find all the taste, smell, touch—all the senses—they have limited capacity to enjoy. After awhile, they get tired of it, and so the joy seems to disappear from life. But if we look for something more than this, deep within us, the very source from where the life has come—that is the source of unceasing joy, continuous stream of joy. That is called bliss.

"Bliss is what? That joy which doesn't bring tiredness, but which makes you more energetic and more alive and more in the moment...

"It's simple. Not that Divine is opposed to life. It's not opposed to life. Divine is not opposed to eating or drink-ing or listening to music or seeing good sights. It's not opposed to anything. It's in fact nourishing to life. It sup-ports life, brings it up. Makes life more interesting.

"Love of God is so intoxicating, such an intoxication. All the past, whatever—pains and rubbishness in the past—

they all get burned down…"

Presumably his words refer to the blend of sensory and silent experience that graced the earlier part of the evening. He proceeds, on a more practical note, to encourage us to take plenty of rest after our travels, inquire whether we are all comfortable in our rooms, invite latecomers to avail themselves of food in the kitchen, etc. He concludes with a silent gaze that seems to take into account every person and every detail in the room. "Good, good," he says, and jumps up from his seat introducing a final chant to be enthusiastically taken up by the group: *"Radhe Govind, Radhe Govind, Radhe Govinda Bhajo Radhe Govind…"*

Seeing that many of us are following Guruji toward the door, a course leader takes command of the microphone and requests everyone to stay for a few important announcements. These prove to be of a logistical nature: where to be by when, how to recognize and prevent altitude sickness, etc. I wander over to a table where I notice that the Question and Botheration Baskets have already been set out, along with pens and paper. I pick up a supply of the paper and make my way, through a sequence of affectionate hugs, out the door and back to my room.

The bhajans of the evening are pleasantly sailing through my mind as I drift off to sleep, and still there when I wake up in the morning. During my shower, one of my roommates has to ask me to stop singing because I am disturbing her meditation. Typically, I have been chanting aloud without realizing it. My own morning meditation seems to be more concerned with bhajans than with my mantra—another familiar experience. Guruji often speaks, as he did last evening, about the love of God being "such an intoxication." Perhaps this is just the way all my "past rubbish" is "getting burned down."

Still, I find myself questioning, for the umpteenth time, whether my mind's recurrent obsession with chanting might not be a completely healthy thing. As I wait for the morning meeting to begin, I pen an expression of this concern and drop it into the Question Basket. The "inner game of Russian roulette" has resumed.

The early part of the day, after yoga asanas and breath work, is devoted to what I would describe as shared self-perception exercises. Our course leaders call them simply "processes." So far as I can discern, they serve basically two purposes: a mental purpose of getting us started in the direction of inward observation and inquiry, and a social purpose of bonding, so we will feel at ease with the people we are about to spend several days not talking to. By mid-afternoon, we are committed to the protocol of the full silence regimen, and gliding into the deep waters of Gurudev's personally guided "Hollow and Empty" meditations.

After dining in silence, our chanting assumes a more soulful demeanor, by comparison to the high energy of yesterday evening. Even the drummers sound melodious. When Guruji opens his eyes, he immediately reaches for the Question Basket, which has been moved to its official position on a low table next to his chair. My heart flutters as I wonder whether my contribution will be among those chosen for reading aloud. This is a new development: I can't recall ever before feeling so nervous about the prospect of my questions getting read and answered. My anxiety evidently has no power to protect me from whatever it is I fear, for my note becomes one of his first selections:

"Dear Gurudev,

"I have fallen in love with bhajans. But I have some questions about how to best use them in my life. I find that very often when I sit to meditate, bhajans go through my mind instead of my mantra. I apply the instructions for correct meditation, but the charm of the bhajan seems to be giving more serious competition to the charm of experiencing finer states of the mantra, than other kinds of mental activity do. I have been meditating for twenty years, and deeply rely upon my regular dive into deep transcending. I am concerned with the quality of my meditation practice.

"I also find that during my daily activity, bhajans keep going through my mind very persistently. It is quite blissful, but is there some reason for concern about dividing my mind? I feel I need some guidance on these points."

The person given the job of reading my question happens to be the professional singer with the powerful voice. She obviously relishes the prospect of Gurudev discoursing upon a musical theme, and delivers my words and phrases "with feeling." It creates a slightly humorous effect, producing a chuckle here and there in the room as she reads. Nevertheless, I feel grateful for the moral support of her lively enthusiasm.

Guruji's response takes a slightly different direction than either she or I might expect:

"Bhajans are wonderful, but don't overdo anything." The abrupt and somewhat deflating point, coming directly after the reader's fulsome rendition, provokes a wave of laughter from the group.

"You know," he continues, "we have this tendency of overdoing. Milk is very good, but if you drink it a lot, it can cause you diarrhea." This time I have to laugh along with the rest. So what if the laughter is partly at my expense? At least, he is definitively answering my question!

"In the same way, you keep singing the bhajan, no problem, you enjoy it; but at the end of every bhajan, or after singing some bhajans, sit in silence, and see how the mind quietens.

"See, both are essential, hmm? Silent transcending is essential. And the bhajans are there for that. Takes you to a peak and then brings you down to that depth of silence. Hmm? Good, good."

It is practical, straightforward advice, delivered in a respectful, sensitive, eye-to-eye manner. I'm certainly not being flattered; but I definitely am, once again, being honored. I feel validated for acting upon the instinct that prompted me to ask the question. In fact, Guruji obviously agrees that there is something less than completely healthy amongst all the bliss I am experiencing. I am eager to see for myself how it works to apply the simple solution of consciously chosen silence to my frustrating tendency toward devotional "diarrhea," and mentally review the details of the instruction so that hopefully I won't forget to use them when the situation arises.

Like a child exploring a new toy, these thoughts so preoccupy me that I completely space out on the next few questions. But the final two notes of the evening address subject matter which deeply interests me:

Question: "Is God both personal and impersonal?"

Sri Sri: "The moment you say 'God,' it has become personal. If you want to experience it as impersonal, you call it just 'energy.' Energy is impersonal. Say, the creative energy, or the cosmic energy, is impersonal. But the moment you utter the word 'God,' it's already personal, no?"

Question: "I have heard that a man is ego wrapped around ego. When we drop our ego, what is left?"

Sri Sri: "Hollow and empty." The cleverly succinct reference to our informal nickname for his guided meditations provokes another round of laughter, and deftly underscores the point he wishes to elaborate:

"Ego simply means unnaturalness, wanting to show off. 'I am somebody great;' 'I am somebody wonderful;' 'I am somebody very intelligent;' 'I am higher than you;' I am more evolved than you.' All these things creating a barrier between you and everyone else, is ego. Being natural, just like a child, and feeling one with everyone, having a sense of belongingness with everybody, whether you know them or you don't, is egolessness. Very simple."

At this point, he closes his eyes as if to assert that we have come upon an appropriate emphasis with which to end the day. After a moment or two, he pushes the microphone away and stands up, introducing one more melodious chant. We also arise, in honor of his departure, singing in response to his lead and spontaneously clearing an aisle through which he slowly progresses, exchanging smiles and eye contact with various individuals along the way.

Guruji's final chant is soaring through my mind as I silently exit the hall. Impulsively, I decide to take a walk before retiring, and wander outside to the old swimming pool. The high-pitched drone of the insects in the grass offers sympathetic accompaniment to the melodies dancing in my head, as I sit down with my feet dangling over the edge of the dry basin and gaze up at an invisible God, whether personal or impersonal, among the stars.

"The moment you say 'God,' it has become personal," he said. So is it we, then who call forth a personal dimension from the Ultimate Reality, simply by addressing it as God? And has humankind been doing this, throughout the ages the world over, in our yearning to bring closer That which we cannot but adore – only to become entangled in absurd and tragic squabbles over whose Name of God is really true? On the other hand, does it even matter whether my incessant songs of praise are offered to a personal God, or to "just the cosmic creative energy?" Isn't adoration a natural human response, either way?

The harmonies of inner and outer music become intolerably immense. My heart swells full to bursting and tears begin to flow from my eyes. I wipe them away on my sleeve, smiling apologetically at my own emotional excess, and observing that even in solitude I am still embarrassed to cry. My mind stands poised for an instant on the brink of a melancholy re-run through the early childhood origins of my inhibitions about crying, then resolutely turns away. So what if I am embarrassed? This feeling of embarrassment itself is such a sweet and tender thing! Whereupon my tears flow anew and the bhajans surge triumphantly through my swimming brain.

The bards of our brave New Age counsel to "follow your bliss." My heart is indeed choosing bliss at every turn, but so often the current seems to be gushing out of control. "Devotional incontinence," I think, laughing ruefully over my condition. "Gurudev is right. This really is somewhat like diarrhea."

I make a conscious effort to recollect his words: *"Takes you to a peak, and then brings you down to that depth of silence."* Perhaps this would be a good time to try out his instructions.

I stand up and begin to move with the music in my mind, twirling and dancing and waving my arms as if conducting my own private universe of celestial and terrestrial strummers. As my imaginary symphony retires from the summit of its natural finale, I bow to my co-star lizards and crickets and cicadas, resume my seat at the edge of the empty pool, and close my eyes, choosing silence. My breath and heartbeat settle into quietude; the murmur of the insects fades away; and the indescribable calm of transcendence immerses me wholly.

Some time later, a particularly assertive cricket intrudes into my void. In unthinking obedience, as if the little noisemaker must be a messenger sent from God, I arise and return to my room. Feeling ephemeral, like a peaceful ghost retiring from its nocturnal watch, I tiptoe noiselessly past my three slumbering roommates, snuggle into my pallet on the floor, and sleep.

Ananda Mouse

In the morning I feel calm and simple—until the group yoga session, which stirs up some more of my blissy craziness. I keep spacing out on the leader's instructions as my brain soars away on a song. It appears to be no great loss: my tight hamstrings are groaning in rebellion against many of the postures, anyway. Plus, it gives me a few more opportunities to practice choosing silence after my mind has become satiated with a chant. I like the sense of poise and centeredness this is giving me *vis a' vis* my inner life, and wonder if Guruji might have similarly helpful advice to offer about managing "divinely crazy" outward behavior. I still feel a little uneasy about that hand-kissing incident. During the break after yoga, I compose a note about this and drop it into the basket.

The rest of the morning is devoted to deepening our silence through breath work and meditation. As I take my lunch under a shady tree by the pond in the garden and watch the colorful fish, my mind returns to the puzzle of God.

From his audiotaped commentaries, I gather that Guruji's definition of God is essentially no different than the one I memorized in third grade at St. Peter's Lutheran School: 'God is infinite, eternal, omnipresent, omniscient, omnipotent, absolute Being; and God is Love.' But what exactly is the relationship between Gurudev and God?

Some devotees seem to relate to Guruji as if he were also omnipotent, omniscient, omnipresent, etc. Of course, I am quite aware that realized individuals often do possess supernormal abilities, which might include anything from highly developed intuition to healing powers to believe-it-when-you-see-it skills like levitating and manifesting rare-metal amulets out of thin air. But to what extent, and under what circumstances, is it really appropriate to apply to them for supernormal solutions to everyday personal challenges? After lunch, I contribute another note to the basket.

Guruji opens the afternoon meeting by reaching for the Question Basket. Once again my heart flutters nervously, and once again my anxiety is to no avail. My last question becomes the first note he hands to the reader:

"Dearest Gurudev,

"In previous courses with you, and also on some tapes I have heard, people have been asking you to take away their fears, guilt, shortcomings, etc.; and your responses are usually, maybe even always, along the lines of, 'Yes, I have taken them all,' 'They are already gone,' etc. I was brought up to pray to God in a similar manner; and I am wondering, is there any difference between what you are doing in response to appeals of this nature, and what God would do? Is it appropriate to disburden oneself of absolutely anything in this manner, or are there some kind of limitations? There are definitely a few things in my life I could use some help with. In any case, I adore you."

Sri Sri: "All the stars are here." In the broad daylight of early afternoon, this is a truly mysterious non sequitur. Does he mean that our group includes all of his most brilliant and illustrious devotees? Does he mean that the Ascended Masters or some category of celestial luminaries has honored us with their invisible presence? Whatever the case, he chooses not to elaborate, but returns to the address of my question with an answer that sends me spinning:

"Hmm? What is God? Somebody sitting up in the heaven? Is that what is your idea of God? What is God?"

My mind explodes in protest against the unflattering implications of the rhetorical question. 'Of course not!' it sputters. 'Surely Guruji must be perceptive enough to know that my concept of God is more sophisticated than that!' And yet, as his answer proceeds, I realize that he is only mirroring for me a yawning discrepancy between my thoughts and feelings about this mystery called God:

"God is the lively presence, no? God is everywhere, like the sky..."

It is a relief to hear him affirm how I actually think of God. But it also underscores his point that the very nature of my question exposes a less mature orientation. There is a part of me that is still relating to the Great Grey-Bearded Grandsire on the ceiling of the Sistine Chapel, who after a six-day orgy of creative genius, has retired to his throne above the clouds where he spends his eons basking in the praises of the heavenly hosts and occasionally uttering stern menaces to banish the faithless denizens of Hell to eternal damnation in the broiling bowels of the earth. In short, Gurudev is showing me that an absurdly simplistic notion of God as the Ultimate Ego-Tripper still holds sway over regions of my inner life!

My mind reels from fury to hilarity, and floods of insight come rushing in: 'What a joke! My concepts of God are speaking the truth to me, but they remain only as concepts, perhaps because I learned them at a time when my developing ego needed a God whom ego could understand. Now my God of Ego literally makes no sense and yet continues to claim my loyalty, while my sophisticated concepts beguile me into believing that I have sagaciously put away such childish things. But amidst all this mind stuff, Divine Reality is nowhere to be found. Instead, like the proverbial thief in the night, it comes to me in stealthy forms, through the no-mind of transcendence, through the inexplicable charm of the master's darshan. Now my heart has found, but my mind remains lost. My heart is lost in the embrace of her Beloved and knows only the lays of adoration and praise, while my mind wanders dazedly through veils of concept and illusion…'

"…And when you become hollow and empty," Sri Sri continues, "*you* are not there. What is there is all just the Divine.

"Now this is like the wall and the window. The sky is behind the wall as much as it is behind the window. It's not any way less. The sun is not any way less behind the wall, or more I front of the window. Sun is the sun.

Ananda Mouse

"But when the wall has become transparent, like the window, like the glass, so hollow, so empty, so hollow, so empty, it is able to let the sun shine through. See that? You can see the sky through the window. You cannot miss it. But through the wall it is difficult to see the sky.

"But sky is the same; it's everywhere. That's what it is. Divine is everywhere. So you polish. You become hollow and empty, hollow and empty. You see you are not different, in any way different. You are one with the Divine."

His words ring crystal clear and true. Of course, one whose heart is overflowing with the lively presence of Divine Love, which is God, and whose mind knows only the wisdom of that which the heart has found, could not but be a conduit of Grace to other souls. But I feel humbled and undeserving of his second-person exposition. Does he seriously imagine *I* could become like *him?*

Leaving me no time to speculate, he immediately hands my other question to the reader:

"Dear Gurudev,

"Thank you for your very helpful answer to my question about bhajans last evening. Directing my mind into a few minutes of silence after it has enjoyed a bhajan really seems to help me keep a better balance. This gives me courage to try to ask another question: How to handle unexpected upsurges of bliss?"

The reader has to pause for a wave of laughter from the group. The combined effects of extended meditation and the thin air of the altitude are giving us a trigger-happy funny bone. As our turbulence subsides, he reads on:

"I had an experience on my last course with you as follows: After the Hollow and Empty session, I noticed I was feeling very blissed out. But I had some service to do which required a lot of focus, so I put the bliss in the back of my mind as I went into activity. I was vaguely aware of exceptionally enjoying my *seva*, when a fellow server, who likes to tease me, came by and started kidding me about making too much noise. (My service required some talking.)

"I should say that I always just love it anyway when this particular friend kids with me, because his manner reminds me of my father's teasing when I was a little girl. On this occasion, my friend jokingly put his hands over my mouth, and I experienced that suddenly my bliss broke through uncontrollably, and I found myself wildly kissing his hands..."

Even the reader loses it at this point, as we all launch into the beginning stages of a laughing binge. Catching a moment in between waves of hilarity, he manages to insert my next sentence:

"When I became aware of what I was doing, I thought, 'Oh, dear God! I could be giving this friend the wrong idea!"

Laughter again rages out of control, and the reader once again has to find a chance to insert another sentence. He raises his voice so as to better be heard:

"I broke away and ran to the bathroom."

For some reason this sentence pulls out all the stops, and the inhabitants of the room go collectively crazy until nearly everyone runs out of breath, whereupon the reader is able to continue:

"I just shook myself. It was like I was literally drunk. I splashed cold water on my face and pulled myself together, and then went out to resume my service, feeling very shook up and concerned about my behavior. My friend showed no signs of any misunderstanding, fortunately.

"I now notice that so far on this course, I am a little bit guarded with myself during Hollow and Empty." Our laughter threatens to erupt again, but the reader forestalls it by raising his voice slightly, and keeps on going: "I know that this is because I am still a little shook by what I did. I have listened again to all of your Bhakti Sutra tapes, and you did mention on one of them that with your master you sometimes had to not express your bliss because the other people couldn't understand. Could you go into this process a little more deeply? I feel a need for a little reassurance that I will be able to keep my behavior more or less within the channels that are appropriate to the relationship in question."

A quieter round of chuckles and giggles greets my closing remark, then subsides into expectancy as Gurudev pauses before answering:

"Hmm? Doesn't matter if it happens once or twice. You have something to laugh at, and remember...Hmm?" His voice is smilingly soft and tender, but his eyes are twinkling with amusement as he gives me a sweet encouraging glance and then signals the reader to proceed with the next question.

The sheer common sense of his response transports me into wonderment. His understated manner of relating to my inner and outer craziness feels so gratifying, and yet runs so unexpectedly contrary to the 'Dear Abby' wisdom of the world. Surely, if I were to take myself to a conventional therapist, my aberrant external behavior would be deemed the appropriate focus of intervention. The excesses of my inner experience might also be attended to (subdued with drugs or analyzed for clues to unresolved trauma), but even this would be for the purpose of enabling me to keep my external behavior within appropriate boundaries. And in compliance with the consensus of our time, the wording and motivation of my appeal to Gurudev reflects this same overriding concern with maintaining externally appropriate behavior.

But in Guruji's approach, the quality of my inner experience is the chief focus of concern; and the gentle self-discipline of consciously chosen silence is suggested, not to subdue or analyze, but to balance and deepen it. My outright behavioral aberration, on the other hand, is almost light-heartedly dismissed: presumed unlikely to recur more than "once or twice," and to merit nothing heavier than indulgent laughter and fond remembrance. It is such obviously practical, sensible advice; and at the same time, so astonishing! With a single stroke he has (once again) disassembled and realigned my personal parameters of sanity.

But even more compelling is the way his answer tacitly affirms and validates the moments of ecstasy that some-times arise in my life, imposing not so much as a whisper of caution or restraint against being overtaken by them. It is an invitation to relax from denying, even to myself, how much I secretly cherish them when they grace my experi-ence; and for this I am melting at his feet.

Eventually, my attention returns to the last few questions being read and answered. As he speaks, I continue to mar-vel at the effortless authenticity with which he administers his gentle wisdom:

Question: "Now during silence I have noticed two distinct voices inside my head. The first is a childlike voice, looking for others' reactions and approval, feeling jealous and left out, and wanting attention. The other voice is a critical voice, sternly disapproving of the unenlightened needs of the childlike person inside. Are these both ego? I feel so uncomfortable with these two voices fighting inside my head. I offer you this tiresome duo. Can you comment?"

Sri Sri: "Good, you have become aware of it first. That's already half done. Do not resist it or try to repair it. You know? Your trying to correct it makes you be with it all the time. Just ignore it, like so many thoughts floating in the mind. Hmm? Look into your nature. You are much more than all these little chatterings."

Question: "Could you say something about a master's darshan—the value of it, how it works, how a disciple can gain the most benefit? Does it develop Divine Love?"

Sri Sri: "See, look at the mind behind that. The mind wants to gain something. 'What will I gain? What will I gain? How will I be benefited?' What is that you want to be benefited? What is that you want to gain? Hmm? Suppose you become the lord of the whole world, what will you do? Set it right? Look into all the problems? What is that you want to gain? Hmm?

"A darshan is not to gain something; it's to lose yourself. Master does not give you something, but he removes all the illusion that you are carrying on in your head that blocks you from being in your heart. See? All that falls off. All the illusion, the karma, they just drop away. You become more hollow and more empty. Hmm? And the irony is, that's when you get everything. It is when you lose all that, then you gain everything.

"But if you are in a 'wanting to gain,' then you will never be hollow and empty. You see what I am saying? It's a process of dissolving, disappearing, rather than achieving. Whatever you achieve will always be smaller than you, because the achievement is of the small ego, small 'i.' Hmm?"

With unrelenting patience, he is gently, sensitively, respectfully enticing, teasing, turning us—away from

limited boundaries, identifications, perspectives, achieve-
ments, and toward the unbounded dimensions available to
human experience: "You are much more than all these little chatterings." "Whatever you achieve will always be
smaller than you…" His words are so lightly, yet firmly
uplifting, like gentle breezes transporting us on eagle
wings.

And transporting us not only through knowledge, but
also, for the remainder of the afternoon, through the
direct experiences of meditation, as he deftly steers our
course beyond the territorial domains of self. In guiding
our silent, inward journeying, every detail of physical, sen-
sational, conscious life becomes like a rivulet or stream
emptying into the vast and hollow ocean of immensity,
universality, infinity, nonentity.

After our meditation, I glide through the waning of this
day in the hallowed space of ineffable contentment, temporarily liberated from the inner drama of concept and
inquiry. Even my mind's preoccupation with chanting subsides into stillness—except for one phrase of liturgical
poetry that resurfaces from the ritual of worship I observed
every Sunday morning for most of the first two decades of
my life: "May the Peace of God, which passes all understanding, keep your heart and mind…" I don't remember
the exact words of the rest of the blessing, but this frag-
ment seems to express the complete truth of an infinitely
perfect and deeply comforting present reality.

Guruji's discourse of the evening takes the form of an

extended response to a single inquiry:

Question: "I often feel that I have old emotional things stored in different layers of my body. Can you please speak about what helps to release these stored emotions? Sometimes I recognize that they are there, but I don't know how to release them, or I am reluctant to do so."

Sri Sri: "Now, don't try to release them. Just observe and be with them. Go through this process (referring to the content of his guided meditations)...With the breath and awareness we are polishing the system... Automatically they get erased and released. Do not resist, and observe those emotions just like any other object. You feel a block —just look at it like a block: 'This is an object.' And you'll see it transforms—its energy goes up.

"You see, in the forehead, something transforms, hmm? Suppose we start with anger: What happens? You are angry. When the anger cools down a bit, you feel sad, because the same anger brings the sadness in the throat. The sensation now, from the eyebrow center, has fallen into the throat. So you are sad, you are unhappy, because you were angry. Now because you are unhappy, and you were angry, now it drops down to your chest, and you feel hatred. Or, you are afraid..."

He is referring to an astute analysis of body/mind energetics, in which specific positive emotions are associated with the upward flow of energy through specific centers of the body, and correspondingly specific negative emotions are associated with the downward flow of energy through the same bodily centers. He seems to assume that most of us are already familiar with this from listening to his Bhakti Sutra commentary; and in my case, he is right. As a body-work practitioner, my professional interest in the subject has prompted me to commit the basic outline to memory:

There is one life-energy that takes different forms in different regions of the body:

As the life-energy moves through the center at the base of the spine, the upward flow is experienced as an awakening of interest in life; and the downward flow is experienced as dullness or inertia.

As the life-energy moves through the center located just behind the genitals, the upward flow is experienced as creative energy, and the downward flow is experienced as sex energy and the urge to procreate.

*As the life-energy moves through the center located just above and behind the navel, the upward flow is experienced as joy and generosity, whereas the downward flow becomes arrogance, jealousy, greed, or a sense of loss.

As the life-energy moves through the heart center, the upward flow becomes love; and the downward flow becomes fear or hatred.

As the life-energy moves through the throat center, the upward flow becomes gratitude, and the downward flow becomes grief or sadness. As it moves through the center located between the eyebrows, the upward flow becomes alertness; and the downward flow becomes anger.

In the center located at the top of the head there can be no downward flow. Life-energy arising to here will be experienced only as bliss.

Gurudev draws upon this system as a framework to assist in the practice of observing. "Observing" involves, in his words, "removing one's identity from the action, from the thought, from the feeling." In this process, a natural sequence comes into play: "Action is gross; thought is subtler; feeling is even subtler; but we are beyond the feelings." Since feelings are in a sense closer to where we are, we have a particular tendency to identify with them. But we can more easily remove our identity from them when we understand them as simply "one energy that manifests in various ways."

The value of the practice of observation is that it releases and removes "blocks" in the system. "When you observe, that which is negative falls off, disappears. That which is evolutionary grows up richer and richer. If you observe love, love grows. If you observe fear, fear falls. If you observe joy, joy increases. If you observe jealousy, jealousy disappears."

As part of his instruction, Guruji emphasizes that we "don't try to eliminate negative emotions. The only way to eliminate them is to transform them. They are not a 'stuff.' They are just energy going down…They are not another entity to go away. It is just a transformation of the same energy."

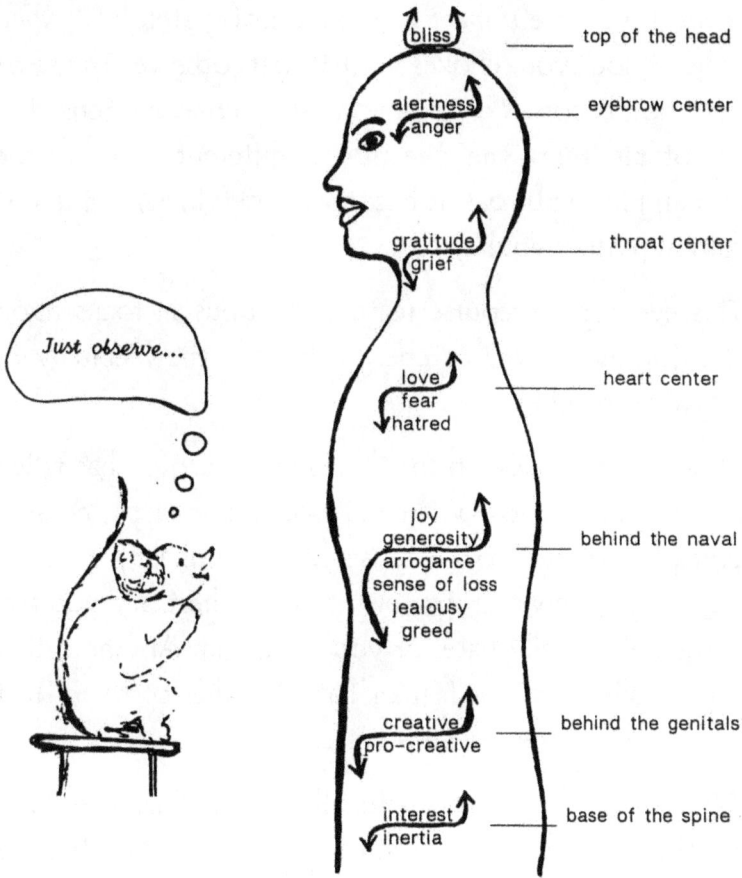

Gurudev further explains that the positive and negative emotions associated with any given energy center cannot simultaneously coexist. "You will not have fear when you have love. When you have fear, you will not have love. And if you are grateful, you will not be sad. You won't be sorry. If you are unhappy, you are not grateful. So when sorrow clogs you, chokes your throat, observe. The same sensation becomes gratefulness. Same sensation. Sensation is not different. The direction is different. Observe the choking in the throat: It becomes gratefulness, and gratefulness purifies your system…"

This evening's discourse features an unusual focus upon the downward flow of energy through the hierarchy of negative emotions:

"The sensation now, from the eyebrow center, has fallen into the throat. So you are sad, you are unhappy, because you were angry. Now because you are unhappy and you were angry, now it drops down to your chest, and you feel hatred. You really hate, or you are afraid. Anything that brings sadness causes fear or hatred, either of them. If it causes hatred, then there is no fear.

"You know, people who hate, all the criminals, they have no fear. But the hatred is strong in them. When there is fear, you don't hate, because you don't act, also. And you will not love, also. Neither love nor hatred is there when fear is there. When hatred is there, there is neither fear nor love. You see that?

Ananda Mouse

"Now the same thing drops down to the navel. When it drops down, what happens? You feel jealous. Whatever you are afraid of, fear causes jealousy, because somebody else is not afraid. It needs the other…Like this, the emotion goes on, all the unpleasantness comes round.

"What do we do now? We just observe. When we look at it, what happens? The negative thing falls apart, and you move up to the next place… The emotions get transformed as sensations in the body… And when you observe the sensations, sensations dissolve—without getting back into emotions. You see this?

"This is a cycle. Emotions create sensations. Sensation creates emotion. So it's a vicious circle. You go on this cycle as a continuous circle. This is the cycle of birth and death. Means what? Bondage is what? The emotions created sensations; and you feel sensation, so you feel emotional. Then emotions create sensation, and it goes on like that.

"Instead, when you observe, what happens? This link breaks. That's what is said: 'The fire of knowledge breaks through.' It removes all the karma, all the unpleasantness. So what happens? The unpleasantness is experienced as sensations and relaxes and releases, and you move on further up… Joy in the navel releases, and you come further up, feel the love. Love moves up: gratefulness. And gratefulness moves up: more awareness. And goes to the top of the head: only manifests as bliss. Hmm?"

In working with my clients, I find this knowledge useful for helping them relate constructively to the emotional release that sometimes occurs during bodywork therapy. I am also, of course, using it in relation to my personal experiences, and with generally gratifying results. The transformations of jealousy into generosity, sorrow into gratitude, even anger into alertness, are happening more and more smoothly in daily life as I apply the procedures of removing my identity from negative emotions and observing the sensations associated with them.

However, there are certain situations in which downward flowing emotions tend to overwhelm my powers of observation. I often experience such intense fear in connection with hazardous traveling conditions—icy roads, airplane turbulence, or anything going wrong with my car—that disengaging identity becomes seemingly impossible. On the other hand, this level of fear is typically short-lived, rarely outlasting the exigency that provokes it; and my husband, a laid-back Type B personality who rarely experiences fear at all, has told me he thinks I am making progress in learning to handle it.

Of greater concern is a chronic problem I experience in connection with the downward flowing energy in the center behind the genitals. Ever since the abdominal surgery associated with my miscarriage, I have been prey to surges of overwhelming sexual desire—usually directed toward my husband, but sometimes also to other men. These attractions to other men represent the most challenging struggle of my inner life; and my attempts to apply the practice of observation to them have produced, so far, little perceivable transformation or redirection of second chakra energy.

To make matters worse, certain of the gentlemen in question self-assuredly refuse to believe that, after fourteen years of marriage, I really could still be as attracted to my husband as I obviously am to them, and seem determined to prove to me that I am fooling no one but myself in clinging to my storybook fantasy of lifelong loyalty to my mate. In moments of clarity, my heart shrinks from the thought of waking up next to anyone with such cynical convictions. But mental and emotional clarity are all too often blurred for me by the giddy exhilaration of my tipsy hormones; and I am becoming keenly aware of how dangerously flattering it can be to be aggressively pursued by physically attractive representatives of the opposite sex. Thus far, the love and honor binding me to my husband has deterred me from committing the unthinkable. But I am genuinely concerned that in some unguarded moment someone might draw me into an action that I would forever regret.

The thought of applying to Guruji for help with this intensely personal struggle occasionally crosses my mind; and I find myself considering it again as I silently return to my room after Satsang and prepare for bed. But I am concerned that it might be grossly inappropriate to present such a matter to a saint who began his spiritual vocation at a very young age and has probably been celibate all his life.

It is now a week since I left home for this course; and I am beginning to miss my husband's calm, affectionate masculine energy, always so reassuring to snuggle up to whenever I want encouragement. I haven't fully confided to him the extent to which I am being challenged with respect to maintaining sexual fidelity, but I know he is compassionately aware of this to at least some extent. His patient understanding toward me is truly wonderful, but I can't reasonably expect to rely upon it forever. The need to reclaim control over my energies and restore my sexuality more totally into his keeping stands out as one of the major urgencies of my inner life, but how does one accomplish such a thing? I fall asleep thinking of him with longing, and feeling grateful that at least I am married to a man eminently worthy of the loyalty I am striving to sustain.

The first question Guruji pulls out of the basket the next day reveals that I am not the only person present who is interested in obtaining enlightened advice about sex:

Question: "Must married couples grow into a celibate relationship in order to reach enlightenment? Must they restrict sexual intercourse to only those times when conception is possible? What are the ideal attitudes and sexual practices of married couples seeking maximum evolution and enlightenment? What are the most important things that householders must do to reach enlightenment in this embodiment?"

Sri Sri: "Hmm? Well, I cannot speak; I am not an authority

on that. But I can tell you one thing: What is it that you are looking for in sex? You are looking for bliss, isn't it? Joy. Hmm?

"When you gain so much more bliss, which is more permanent and more everlasting, then the few minutes of physical experience, which leaves you run down and tired a little later on—which you would prefer? When you start preferring something more blissful, something more enjoyable, something more energetic, then you have become a celibate in a natural manner, without suppressing. Celibacy is not something that you practice, forcing yourself into, but something that happens to you in a very natural and spontaneous manner.

"The best example we can think of is the cotton candy. As a child you were so much into cotton candy, weren't you? Or lollipops. Cotton candy means eyes lit up and hands go like this! You want to hold the cotton candy and make it all over the face, mess it up, and eat that—you were in heaven! But did you make an effort to lose interest in cotton candy? You know? Children, you take them to the stalls—they will not move away from the stall once they see it. They get stuck there. The parents would drag them by the hand, 'Come on, let's go!' Right? But now do you do the same thing, when you move through cotton candies, do you get stuck there? You don't even notice it! You have grown.

"Like that, you have had sex so many lifetimes—being a dog, being a horse, being a whatever. In all these animal lives you have had it over and over and over. After eating, this is the second experience, everlasting and so long time. These are the two experiences—eating and sex, and then third comes sleeping—that you have had all the time. So when you move on, then naturally a point comes, a point of saturation, that it doesn't really bother you or interest you anymore, because you are all blissful. That joy and bliss is emanating from every cell of your body. When there is such a vibrant bliss in your body, then you don't look for it. No? That is when celibacy has happened naturally.

"And when you are involved in something creative, then also sex does not bother in your mind so much. Hmm? When there is nothing creative going on, then what occupies the mind is sex, because that has been the oldest habit. You see? Your habits overtake you when you are not engaged in something new and something creative.

"You don't have to think that 'This is bad' and 'This is wrong,' 'This is right.' Just be natural and observe, observe, observe."

In spite of his non-judgmental closing statement, I feel somewhat disheartened. I clearly recall a period of time for myself and my husband when the pleasures of sex do begin to take a back seat to more spiritually progressive and energetically upward forms of intimacy. For several years after the initial honeymoon phase of our marriage, our mutual inclinations toward sex diminish to a remarkable extent, even while we continue to grow more deeply bonded emotionally. We suspect this might be related to our practice of certain advanced TM techniques, but neither Maharishi nor any of his senior teachers ever discuss the subject of sex.

When the TM organization begins to promote the Ayurvedic system of natural health, we find the opportunity to mention our nearly celibate situation to one of their Indian Ayurvedic practitioners. We learn that this gentleman regards celibacy as unnatural for householders. In fact, he counsels us that even "twice a week" is not too much. This comes as somewhat startling advice. Indulging ourselves that often would mean sacrificing our other interests to a greater extent than either of us would care to do. But in the belief that it is better for our health, we undertake to become at least somewhat more sexually active, eventually resulting in the disastrous episode of my one dysfunctional pregnancy.

I cannot regret the experience of carrying a child. Even though they are brief and traumatic, the precious few months of communion with that mysterious unborn soul soften the substance of my heart and redirect my growth in gratifying ways. It is, nevertheless, a bit depressing to learn that my sexual tendencies are probably less evolved now than they have been. But I suppose there is not much use in crying over spilled milk. Anyway, Sri Sri obviously is willing to address the subject of sex; and I am beginning to think seriously about confiding my personal concerns to his wisdom.

My reverie is spacing me out on most of the rest of the day's questions, but the subject of the final item catches my attention:

Question: "Are you a world guru? Or are you a personal guru?"

Sri Sri: "I am nobody. It doesn't matter. But it is up to you. If you think I am just for the world, then you are already isolating yourself away. You are moving away. But if you think I am personally with you, then I am very much personally with you. You see that? It is up to you to look into that. Hmm? If you just think I am for the world and for general, for public, for everybody, you will not have the personal connection with me at all. Never mind if I am for the whole world, or the whole universe, or several more worlds—how does it matter to you?"

This answer implodes like a little bombshell in my mind: So, not only do we from our side make God personal, simply by addressing Him or Her as God; but apparently a similar dynamic applies to having a personal relationship with the master! Mentally reviewing all my years of practicing and teaching meditation prior to meeting Sri Sri, I perceive how for the whole time I am doing exactly what he describes—"isolating myself away" from the master by thinking of him as being here "for the world."

Evidently, maintaining an impersonal distance from Maharishi has in fact been a posture of my choice, even while others around me are making the opposite choice.

What I hear Maharishi say always seems to discourage the personal connection, but maybe that is as much as I am ready to hear at the time. For all along, there are others who do not hear the same discouragement from the same words, perhaps because they perceive the underlying truth that the question of the master's dharma is essentially irrelevant to the question of personal connection.

These are sobering thoughts to ponder. It is said that to get an opportunity to personally connect with a living master is an extremely rare and fortunate thing, coming only once in ever-so-many lifetimes. It would seem that I may have unwittingly blown it once already in this life,—and then been graciously afforded a second chance.

The afternoon meditations are colored for me by a chastened sense of gratitude toward Gurudev. My mind rehearses the memory of my first encounter with him, so playfully yet so compellingly reaching out to me—perhaps realizing that, left to herself, this one is unlikely ever to catch on to the subtler etiquette of making the spiritual connection from her side. No wonder there is so much laughter in his eyes when he looks at me! No wonder, and Thank God! The master would certainly need a sense of humor in handling my case: I commit my blunders so conscientiously!

Of course, I am not the only modern Western aspirant awkwardly fumbling and stumbling through the unfamiliar ins and outs of relating to an Eastern saint. No doubt, many of my fellow course participants are also experiencing uncertainties in this area. In this evening's discourse, Guruji kindly spells out a few more of the basics for us:

"What is that enlightenment which has no love in it? Can there be one such? I don't think so. If it is there, I don't think anybody will go in for it. If there is a sort of desert sort of enlightenment state where there is no love, I don't think anybody would want to have it. At least, we don't know.

"Now, if you consider enlightenment as love for the entire universe, for everybody, for everyone: what is the way? How can you expand like that? You have to begin somewhere. And it's easiest to begin with the master.

"Because everywhere else, you find that there is some demand on you. The moment there is a demand, you withdraw. You give love to those who do not demand from you. The moment somebody seems to look for your love, you seem to go a step back. This is always the case in giving. Someone asks you a lot, you don't feel like giving to them. Someone doesn't ask, you give them presents. The whole world is in this practice.

"If you could not love a master, it's very difficult to love somebody else. Because master is void of any demand, and is unconditionally supporting you. He doesn't say, 'Oh, you are good, so I support you.' 'You are talented, so I support you.' 'You behave this way, so I support you.' No. He says, 'Wherever you are, however you are, I am yours.' That's what a master says: 'I am with you.'

"Master is just like a window. See, the sky is all over. See, the stars are behind the wall as much as they are behind the window. But through the window we can see them; we cannot miss the sky; we cannot miss the stars. That's why they have said it's almost impossible without being this way.

"Now, are the techniques alone sufficient? It's not. Technique alone is not sufficient. Behind the technique is the Grace. It's the Grace that really works. The technique is also important. It has its place, no doubt. But it alone will not do.

"It's like—I usually give this example of a bowl of soup and a spoon. The soup in the bowl is the Grace; and holding the spoon is the technique. If you are holding the spoon upside down, then also you cannot enjoy the soup. But if you are just holding the spoon upright, in the right position, but there is no soup in the bowl; then one thousand times you go between the mouth and the cup and nothing comes into it.

"So both correctness of the technique and the practice, as well as the Grace, are essential."

I find myself once again hearing echoes from the religious teachings of my childhood:

"Though I speak with the tongues of men and of angels, and have not love, I am become as a sounding brass, or a tinkling cymbal. And though I have the gift of prophecy, and understand all mysteries, and all knowledge; and though I have all faith, so that I could remove mountains, and have not love, I am nothing. And though I bestow all my goods to feed the poor, and though I give my body to be burned, and have not love, it profiteth me nothing..." (St. Paul's letter to the Corinthians, Chapter 13)

As I ponder the resemblance between the wisdom that guides my youth, and the wisdom flowing to me now, another piece of the puzzle clicks into place: My spiritual practice, now and for most of my years of adulthood, is focused primarily upon technique. It is quite clear to me how techniques of meditation, breath-work, yoga, etc. are essential to cultivate the capacity, in the physical nervous system, for accessing and sustaining the expansion, the subtlety, the power of transcendental experience. But mere techniques and practice and cultivating of the physiology are in a sense like the "sounding brass" and "tinkling cymbal" of the scripture passage. They are mainly about form, and tell but half of the story.

The other half of the story is about content, the subjective nature of the spiritual experience itself; and the content in question is love. In the religion of my childhood, the ultimate spiritual reality is the eternal, omnipresent God; and "God is love." In the teachings of Gurudev, the ultimate source of all experience, from the finest level of feeling to the grossest level of activity, is transcendental consciousness. And the subjective reality of transcendence turns out to be also love—"unconditional Divine love," love which is "not an emotion; it is our very existence."

And how we know love is through relationship. In the religion of my childhood, one establishes a living relationship with God through Christ—by reading His story in the scriptures, and by participating in the Sacraments of Baptism and Holy Communion. These two—Word and Sacrament—are called "the means of Grace;" i. e., they are the means by which the Grace of God flows into a person's life, transforming negative and sinful tendencies into positive and loving motives and intentions.

In Guruji's explanation, we experience Divine love through a living personal connection with the embodied master or saint, the perfectly clear window through whom Omnipresent Love shines clear and undistorted, touching our hearts and beckoning us homeward to the Kingdom of Heaven within. It is the perennial doctrine of Grace which lies at the mystical center of both Western and Eastern spiritual traditions. In the words of St. Paul, "By Grace are ye saved through faith; and that not of yourselves: it is the gift of God: not of works, lest any man should boast." (Ephesians 2: 8-9) Or, in the words of Gurudev, "It's the Grace that really works."

It is not quite clear to me what is happening here, but I seem to be coming around full circle to what is arguably *the* central theological doctrine of my Protestant upbringing: the doctrine of salvation by Grace. I'm not quite sure I am ready for this. Some of these correspondences between the teachings of my childhood religion and the teachings of Sri Sri are beginning to stir up a cauldron of turmoil between my heart and my mind.

In my youth, I develop an aversion to doctrinal theology, mistrusting it as a form of mind-control with a tendency to erode the very foundations of intellectual integrity. Throughout most of my formal education, all but four years of which take place on church-related campuses, I avoid curriculum theology, substituting independent study alternatives wherever possible. I value above all the right and the freedom to consider any idea however unorthodox, and to be true to my own innate sense of what is convincing and what is not. I endeavor to preserve my intellectual autonomy as far as possible from the potentially compromising tentacles of a'priori belief systems vying for my adherence upon such purely strategic bases as heritage and family connection. I habitually regard most theological doctrines with profound skepticism, suspecting that many of them have only come into existence at all as surreptitious means for organizing people's loyalties around political and economic agendas. I am also aware that there is much in modern Biblical scholarship which supports my skeptical orientation.

And yet, there is something seductively comforting about encountering a major doctrinal tenet of my childhood faith in the teachings of my dear and revered Gurudev. My mind, well trained in the art of protecting her integrity by conscientiously regarding nothing as sacred, perceives this comfort with a wary eye. Am I being lulled into just another form of slavish orthodoxy here?

My heart, however, is proving to be the more powerful rebel: No squeamish mental reservation is going to stop her from entering into the irresistible mysteries of the sacred realm. And so what if Guruji's teachings turn out to be here and there similar to the teachings of Christ and the Apostles? Maybe just goes to prove that there is nothing new under the sun!

I sense that the skeptical powers of my mind are at least temporarily losing ground before the impetuous intentions of my infatuated heart. This produces an unfamiliar tilt in my internal balance of power. My thoroughgoing intellect is not accustomed to being so peremptorily upstaged.

Despite the abundance of rest and meditation in our course routine, heavy waves of fatigue overtake my system in the evening. I know this is not abnormal. Extended meditation alters metabolism in a manner conducive to detoxification of the body, as very deep levels of stress and tension get released. And no doubt the mental and emotional intensity involved in grappling with my unresolved issues around sex and religion would be a contributing factor. In addition, I am experiencing occasional moments of vertigo due to the unaccustomed altitude.

Our course leaders are constantly reminding us that the best preventive measure for both vertigo and uncomfortable detox is the same: Drink water. I realize that I probably am not drinking enough during the night, so I decide to fill up a big jar of purified water after Satsang and keep it by my bed. I intend to write a note to Guruji this evening, regarding the problem of managing my sexual energy. But the simple task of filling my jug and carrying it to my room so exhausts me that further effort of any kind is totally out of the question. Almost before my head touches the pillow, I collapse into a stuporous sleep.

I awake feeling incredible. My heart is as light and fluid as a bubble, and the mere sight of sunshine streaming in through my window brings tears of gratitude to my eyes.

But something is odd. Why is everything so quiet? I look about and realize that I am completely alone in the room. What time is it, anyway? I fumble for my watch and learn that I have overslept by several hours. I shower hastily, and manage to get myself up to the meeting hall in time for the tail end of the morning meditations.

As our attention turns toward lunch, one of the course leaders announces that Sri Sri wants us to practice a particular technique while eating, which might enable us to access and release some past-life *samskaras*, or impressions. The practice involves moving the jaw in a slow circular motion, which the course leader briefly demonstrates. Feeling somewhat giddy and off-balance, perhaps due to my belated entry into the day's routine, I have to repress an irreverent impulse to laugh during the leader's demonstration.

I silently take my place in the lunch line, which for once seems to be moving faster than its usual snail's pace.

However, it appears that the only item on the menu today is an undressed salad composed mainly of shredded cabbage—served out of deep bucket-like pots instead of the usual oversized salad bowls. This irks me. After the first day of the course, I have been skipping both dinner and breakfast to avoid having to rush through my rather lengthy personal meditation routine; so by lunchtime I am always pretty hungry. A meal of nothing but raw cabbage hardly measures up to my stomach's expectations.

I quell my misgivings philosophically, reflecting that a day of raw food fasting might actually even intensify my already wonderfully deep meditations, and proceed to practice the demonstrated jaw movement while chewing. But the irreverent impulse to laugh resurfaces, rendering the practice physically impossible to perform. The nature of the meal, along with the bucket-like vessels it is being served from, seems so suggestive of the feeding of livestock on my father's farm! I find myself wondering if Guruji might be simply playing a practical joke on us. These thoughts provoke such irrepressible laughter that I feel obligated to remove myself from earshot of the others who are silently and absorbedly rotating their jaws around the cabbage.

I try to reason with myself. After all, as a bodyworker I know how profoundly jaw movement is connected with neck tension, which is where some of the stubbornest stress in the body is frequently held. It seems quite possible that in a context of contemplative transcendence, focused, repetitive jaw movements could become a means to access and release past-life samskaras. But every time I attempt to soberly apply the instruction, the thought of Guruji playing a mischievous practical joke lures me into hysterics. By the time I empty my bowl, I have to really compose myself in order to return it with appropriate decorum to the dishwashing station.

As I return my dish, I see that a second course, consisting of soup and bread, has been set out. I decide that a day of raw food fasting probably isn't such a good idea after all, given my light-headed state, and help myself to hearty servings of the hot and nourishing food. But I make no further attempt to apply the jaw rotating technique. Whatever that is about, I have had enough!

After lunch, we are instructed to write down our experiences with the technique and put them into the basket. I mentally gulp, feeling caught in the act of committing a kind of spiritual truancy. Dear God in Heaven, what am I going to say?

Well, you don't lie to the master; so I suppose I just have to confess the truth. I compose a note beginning, "Dear Gurudev, I'm afraid you lost me on this one," and proceed to relate my experience. But I can't summon the courage to put it into the basket, at least not quite yet.

A number of responses are read and discussed during the afternoon meeting. Many, noting the bucket-like serving vessels and grass-like fare, contribute humorous notes about feeling like cows chewing their cud in the pasture. One person simply writes, "Moo." To these, Guruji replies, "That is what you did one whole lifetime, many lifetimes, just chewing, day and night, did nothing but chewing and chewing and chewing. One whole lifetime!" It appears that the object of the exercise may be simply to bring our awareness to the primordially ancient experience of consuming food, thereby loosening some of our attachment to the impressions and expectations surrounding it.

Certain participants, however, write about slipping into hauntingly familiar yet other-worldly scenes. With these responses, Guruji seems particularly delighted. Apparently he has, in fact, been playing a kind of joke on us, but that does not mean that the experiences of those who innocently "fall for it" are not authentic. On the contrary, the element of innocent faith in these exceptional cases becomes a demonstration for the rest of us, of how surrender and trust can call forth the Grace even when the master's intentions may be going in a different direction. It seems that a bogus "technique," even though formulated to be a playful prank, actually becomes an avenue into past-life experience for those who innocently believe in it!

In the course of Gurudev's discussion, it begins to appear highly ambiguous whether the joke is really on those who take the instruction seriously, or on those who perceive it as a joke. In fact, it never becomes completely clear whether a placebo technique is producing bona fide results through the innocent faith of the few, or whether an authentic technique is being mischievously presented in a trick context that tempts most of us to egotistically imagine we are second-guessing the master, thereby sabotaging the subtle interplay of practice, Grace, and faith.

As for myself, I am not even sure which category to identify with. I suppose that my tendency toward hysterical laughter in connection with the technique may boil down to nothing more than the silliness of irreverent egotism. But on the other hand, the same symptoms might be some kind of emotional release triggered by my basically sincere attempts to practice a potent technique properly. At any rate, considering my cowardice about contributing my experience to the basket at all, I don't think I can claim to have passed any test of faith.

The one thing that seems clear to me is that a "mischievous prank" is being employed as a brilliant teaching device, creating a memorable learning experience for everybody. Regardless of our individual approach to the instruction, on the entire scale from innocent blind faith to complicated sophistry, the same message about preserving the delicate balance of surrender, Grace, and faith has been compellingly conveyed.

Gurudev's masterful lesson leads me wandering back to the issue of religion, reminding me that the Protestant doctrine of salvation by Grace is often more fully expressed as "salvation by Grace through faith." I note, too, that the latter part of that quote from St. Paul's letter to the Ephesians, which is often cited as the scriptural basis for this doctrine, describes a set of conditions strongly suggesting the posture of surrender: *"By Grace are ye saved through faith; and that not of yourselves: it is the gift of God: not of works, lest any man should boast."*

Quite clearly, both Sri Sri and St. Paul are talking about the attainment of spiritual goals by Grace, through faith, in surrender. Sri Sri would perhaps use terms such as "enlightenment," "the *brahman*," (fully expanded unity consciousness) or "liberation," rather than "salvation," to describe the ultimate object of the spiritual quest. But by "enlightenment," "unity," or "liberation," Sri Sri does mean release from the bondage of separateness imposed by ego-identification. And by "salvation," St. Paul does mean release from the bondage of "sin," which in Christian thought is often defined as the condition of separateness from God due to human egotism…

Meanwhile, Guruji has progressed to answering some of the general questions from the basket. My attention is recalled as he fields a sequence of questions about his relationship with his own master:

"Dear Sri Sri,

"Can you talk about how you knew who your master was? As we were chanting *"Guru Om"* just now, I realized I am still not sure who my master is. Do you choose your master consciously, or does your master choose you, or does it just happen?

Guruji seems to go inward for a moment, and then answers

very quietly, "Hmm? Doesn't matter. When such confusion comes, any amount of explanation or understanding does not satisfy. Just relax and go silent, and in that very silence all answers come through. See that? It becomes so clear, so obvious. Hmm?" He nods for the reader to continue with the next question:

"Sri Sri, how does your master feel about what you are doing?"

Sri Sri: "How do you feel about that?" This, of course, evokes a response of laughter from the group, after which Guruji continues: "You have some doubts? You want some authenticity, some stamp on it? What is that? What is it you are looking for? Hmm?

"I understand. The mind is...there is some conflict that may come: 'Oh, am I not doing the right thing?' Hmm?

"If the doubt still persists, just wait for some time. It will clear by itself. It can cook you. This very doubt can cook you well. You will be ready."

Gurudev might extol the value of faith, but he certainly is not advising us to dismiss, deny, or repress our doubts, not even doubts about himself. I find this tremendously reassuring. One of my chief quarrels with the teachings of my religion is over its insistence upon the need to cling to faith in certain specific beliefs, regardless of questions and doubts that might sincerely arise. Sri Sri, on the other hand, appears to have every respect for the spiritual and intellectual autonomy of the seeker, and to harbor no dogmatic interest in fettering anyone's mind.

The final question of the afternoon returns us to the subject of sex:

"Dear Guruji,

"Yet another sex question: When sexual desire does spontaneously move itself out the window—"

Guruji interrupts to inquire about the meaning of the phrase "out the window" in relation to sexual desire. Amidst waves of general hilarity, the reader attempts to explain what the writer intends to convey; and Guruji eventually gets the idea: "That means, when it is gone?"

"Yes, right," the reader affirms, and then continues to read, "...or out of the way; on what basis do you consummate a relationship with another person? In this culture, sex is definitely a part of relationships, to most people. If one is single now, and sexual desire is on the fence—"

Here the reader, expecting that Guruji would need another explanation, inserts, "That means, 'could go either way with it.'" However, as everyone roars with laughter, he has to retract: "Oh, that's not it, either,"—which only intensifies our hilarity.

Abandoning his ill-fated attempt, the reader returns to the text of the question: ".as a result of spiritual work, does that mean that there may not be a need to be intimate with one special person? Or am I about to enter yet another uncharted world of weirdness where there is even less chance of finding a compatible partner than there is already? What is fun, anyway? Is that out the window, too?"

Guruji joins with us in an uproarious round of hilarity, and then playfully responds, "Is the fun out of the window?"—which elicits yet more laughter, though of a somewhat less raucous nature.

"How can fun be out of the window?" The intonation of his rhetorical expression expresses childlike innocence and incredulity, shifting us into a slightly different angle on the subject:

"Now, you can have fun with anything. Or, you can be miserable with anything. You can be miserable having sex desires. And you can be miserable having no sex desires. Thinking you are abnormal because you don't have sex desires—this may bother you. Do you see that?

"There is much more to life than just the body. There is a lot more. Hmm? And you can have fun. If you want to have fun, you can be happy in spite of anything and without anything. You see that? It is up to you.

"This is not something that you can force yourself on. Forcing sex on you is like—is the other way of suppression. Same thing like suppression.

"But rising above both and seeing that it's nothing much. Going above that. Seeing yourself as moving glow of light, of consciousness, of energy. When you are filled with a lot of prana, a lot of energy, it takes a different color, different dimension.

"So be with whatsoever is at whatever time. Move with it, with this awareness that I am much bigger than all this. Then you will not regret, 'Oh, I do not have the desire,' or whatever.

"In ancient Vedic times, this was a rule, that both husband and wife had to participate in any meditation or any programs together. This was a rule. So that it won't create an imbalance between them. They both had to walk together. And when both come up and both lose the desires, that is the ideal thing. When one loses the desire, and the other still has a lot of it; then it creates a little imbalance there. So it is said, both together should participate, together should come in any religious activity, whether *yagya*, meditation, etc. They were not allowed to come by themselves, but told, 'No, you should bring your spouse and come together, as a householder.' That was wise. It's very logical. Hmm?"

The wording and querulous undertone of this question strike me as almost offensively crude, but Guruji nevertheless honors it with a thorough and sensitive response. And I have to admit that his playfully respectful answer contains a great deal of relevance to my own situation. I obviously am a case in point of someone who can "be miserable having sex desires." There certainly are moments when I need to remember that "there is much more to life than just the body," and that I can choose to be happy even in the midst of a frustrating struggle. I'm not exactly sure how to practice "rising above and seeing myself as a moving glow of

light, of consciousness, of energy" in the heat of a challenging moment; but the idea sounds highly appealing.
The advice to "be with whatsoever is at whatever time" and
"move with it, with this awareness that I am much bigger
than all this" actually feels rather daring to contemplate;
but it is followed by "then you will not regret." Maybe
there is a direction of growth being pointed out here that
I ought to consider more deeply. And Gurudev's comment
about the rule in Vedic times requiring husband and wife
to spiritually move together, clearly has something to say
to my husband and myself.

My personal concerns are by no means entirely resolved by
this discussion, but it does open up several promising
avenues of inquiry; and I have to acknowledge a debt of
gratitude to the person who has risked embarrassment by
contributing this question.

Even though we are still observing silence, this evening's
Satsang is to be open to the public. I join the volunteers
who stay behind, following the afternoon meditations, to
clean and decorate the meeting hall in preparation for the
newcomers. We move our cushions and backjacks around
to one side of the stage, leaving room in the center for
rows of folding chairs. The musicians rearrange their sound
equipment and work out the accompaniment to some
chants that are hopefully easy enough for newcomers to
follow. Most of us dress for the evening with more attention to outward appearance than at any time since our
arrival.

The area organizers have been effective with publicity; and the rows of chairs quickly fill up with eager, wondering, curious faces. The musicians open the evening by leading several simple chants as the guests are welcomed and seated. Many are holding flowers to offer to Sri Sri; and quite a few pick up the available song sheets and join in the chanting. It appears to be an audience somewhat familiar with the general protocol of such events.

One of the course leaders stands up with a microphone and delivers a brief welcoming address, including basic information about Sri Sri Ravi Shankar and his organization, as well as a few words of explanation about our retreat and the traditional regimen of silence that we are observing.

His talk ends as Guruji enters the hall, introducing a chant to be picked up by the musicians, and accepting flowers from every side. Stepping up onto the stage, he hands his armload of flowers to someone who can put them into vases with water, and then sits in his chair and closes his eyes, as usual, for the duration of the chant in progress. At the end of the chant, he smilingly opens his eyes and begins his talk by asking the audience what topics they would like him to discuss. It is an approach he often uses, sure to produce an interesting array of topics, which he can creatively blend into a unique discourse with personal relevance to everyone present.

Still feeling a little light-headed and spacey, as I have for most of the day, I make no attempt to remember the list of topics he gathers, or even to intellectually follow his talk. I feel like taking a break from the mental rigors of self-inquiry, and decide to just relax and enjoy myself by watching Guruji as he relates to the newcomers.

A short while into his discourse, Guruji begins to illustrate some point by telling a story:

"Between two kingdoms, there was long-standing rivalry. They were enemies. But then people advised one of the kings, 'Why have this rivalry and fight all your life? Why not make friends?'

"The king said, 'Alright, okay.' So he sent a picture of himself to the other king, for a present.

"But when the other king got the picture, he was sarcastic. You know, usually when people are rivals or enemies, they don't trust. They don't believe. Even the good will is not believed. So, he didn't believe. He said, 'Okay, where to put this picture?' He thought. Then he said, 'Okay, you put this picture by my toilet.'

"It became a big insult. It's a very big insult to have a picture put in the bathroom! The ambassador who took this message came back and reported to the king; and the king became very furious. He asked his advisor, 'Why did you advise me to send the picture there?'

"But you know, advisors are very intelligent. You know what the advisor said? 'Oh, king, it is very good! That man must be so afraid of your picture, and he may be suffering from big constipation problem. So in the bathroom he looks at your picture, and he may find it very easy there. So he has put…"

At this point, I completely lose it and begin to laugh hysterically. Of course, I am not laughing alone; in fact, the whole room is roaring. But I'm afraid I may be one of the loudest to be heard. I can hardly believe my ears that a spiritual master, representing a venerable unbroken lineage of seers reaching back to the dawn of time, could actually be illustrating a point by telling a story with a punch line about constipation, and to a public audience at that! He is totally blowing my mind.

Guruji regards our hilarity with calm and tolerant amusement; and as it subsides, he steadily continues: "This answer satisfied the king, who was going to wage a war…" His very steadiness in the face of our volatility provokes another uproarious outburst, to which he guilelessly responds, "This was really something that happened. It's not a story. It's a history."

This, of course, sends us into even more outrageous hysteria. But Gurudev has no intention of giving up on making his point, and smilingly continues when he can again be heard: "One adviser, one minister, averted a whole war between two kingdoms, in India, because he said this. This is what the fact is.

"Any situation—otherwise it can explode—or you can turn it to your advantage. You know? Someone tells you, 'You look like a ghost.' You can go on fighting with them: 'How dare you call me a ghost?' In that way the spark triggers, the whole fight begins. Instead you can easily say, 'Yes, I am a holy ghost.'"

This gets us laughing again, but now we are with him, attentively following as he continues to make his point: "Finished. The whole argument finishes there. You know?

"There are these stories in the *Puranas*, in ancient days, that someone shot someone with a bow and arrow: They shoot this arrow, and this weapon came; and the saint just did his hand like this and the weapon became a flower. The weapon, which was going to hit and hurt a person,—just by their look, it turned into a garland, or into a flower. Hmm?

"Somebody is shooting an arrow at you: they are shooting because they are miserable. When you are like a flower, you can turn that into a flower. When you have blossomed from within, any insult—you can take it for your advantage.

"What other insult could there be?—Tell me, give me some example."

Someone in the audience suggests the insult, "Stupid idiot."

Sri Sri: "Say, 'stupid idiot.' This is what people might say. You can say, 'Yes, stupid people make the whole fun in the world. I am happy to make you laugh.' All the fools make the entertainment industry. The most foolish things are when people are laughed at, and people are entertained by that. So you say, 'Yes, I agree. Thank you.'

"Take every insult as a compliment. Every insult can be taken as a compliment. Doesn't matter, you cannot be insulted, cannot be insulted at all. They are simply pouring out the stress or the tension or the anguish or anxiety in them. So you receive it, take it. Hmm?"

Of course, it is not lost on me that Gurudev has just demonstrated precisely the point he is making. Probably I am not the only person present whose attention may have been flagging, or who may have shot subtle arrows of disapprobation at him in response to his colorful story about the two kings in India. A lesser luminary might take offense at either of these slights, thereby triggering a spark of friction between himself and an unworthy audience. But Guruji's approach is to claim our hearts, as well as our attention, by freely allowing us (perhaps even encouraging us) to laugh at what we perceive to be his foolishness. And very likely there may have been "stress or tension or anguish or anxiety" coming up in us, which our hearty laughter has cleared out of the way, thereby transforming us into an attentive and open-minded audience, more worthy to receive his wisdom and Grace.

Guruji further elaborates his theme through a sequence of stories about Buddha and his disciples:

"In Buddha's period, India was very prosperous, very very prosperous. But Buddha made a big joke. He made the monks go and beg alms in front of the homes. Because this was very difficult, to ask for food, especially to those very educated and wealthy people who think they are in control. When you have wealth, you think, 'I am in control. I know everything. I can buy the whole world.' Because Buddha himself was a king, was an emperor; and he had an elite class of disciple.

"So he gave begging bowls into the hands of these people —highly educated, high intellectuals, scholars. The rule is, they should ask only in five houses, and whatever they get, they should eat that. That was very crushing for the ego. This was not common in those days. Nobody used to beg. There was no need to beg, because everybody was prosperous.

"It so happened that, like any new movement is not very much welcomed by the people, Buddha's people were not welcomed, because they were going and asking for alms. So one lady, she came out of the house and she got really angry at this person who comes and asks for alms. So this lady takes the garbage can and pours the garbage into his bowl.

"Some other people got upset: 'Look at this lady! If she can't give, she should have simply said no. But instead of refusing, she poured the garbage into the begging bowl!'

"But this *bhikshu*, this monk, started laughing; and he thanked her. He said, 'At least you had the tendency to give something, doesn't matter whether it is garbage or food. You had the tendency of giving. And all that anger that you were building up for these several days, at least you threw it all with the garbage. You expressed it out, so that now you could be comfortable.'

"When people shout or burst out, you can only thank them: 'Well, thank God, so much was getting built up. It has all come out. Okay now, fine, wonderful.' Hmm?

"I'm not saying we should encourage this tendency in us and always justify that. But when it happens, don't regret it. What do we do? We go on regretting. When we regret, we commit the same error again…"

Gurudev's comments about saints turning arrows into flowers, puts me in mind of the basically spiritual principles underlying the traditional martial arts. The Buddhist monk's friendly response to the lady who threw garbage into his begging bowl also reminds me of Christ's teachings about "turning the other cheek," as well as Mahatma Gandhi's inspired strategy of non-violent revolution. In a final anecdote, Guruji develops his theme even further, offering provocative insights into the enlightened perspective behind the legendary wisdom of transforming opposition through the gentle power of inner peace:

"A man came into the satsang of Buddha. He was so angry, annoyed, he came and spat on the face of Buddha. But everybody else was really shaken by that. This man comes and spits on the face of Buddha, in the crowded congregation! Thousands of people were there, but they could not react, because Buddha was smiling! He just accepted it.

"When he did not react, it gave a shock to this man. Anyway, he went home; but he couldn't sleep that whole night. Something happened. In the very presence of

Buddha, something shook up in him. He comes next day running in and falls at the feet of Buddha, and says, 'Please forgive me. Please pardon me. I don't know what I did, why I did...'

"Buddha says, 'I cannot forgive you.'

"When Buddha says, 'I cannot forgive you,' all the other disciples were even more shocked now: What? Buddha says 'I cannot forgive you,' and this poor fellow is crying! He is weeping, and Buddha says, 'I cannot forgive you!'

"And then Buddha explains: 'See, that man is not here right now. On whomever you spat, neither the man who spat is here, nor the man on whom you spat is here right now. When you have never made a mistake, how can I forgive you even?'

"Buddha lifts him up, embraces him, and teaches him the dharma, the meditation; and he crosses this bondage and becomes free.

"Simple things. When I say, 'Okay I forgive you,' I make you a culprit. Whereas you are not a culprit, the stress in you has been a culprit. And when the stress is gone, who is to be forgiven?

"And it was the stress in one person which thinks another person has done a mistake. So who is the forgiver? And who is to be forgiven? A stress is forgiving the stress!

"When I am rid of stress, I see this only as a game, as a play. Then when there is no winning or losing, whatever is there is just all a game, a play. It's not fight. It's not war. It's fun. Even in play, there is, you can say, 'I won' and 'I lost;' but in fun there is no winning or losing. It's just fun. *Swastino Brihaspati Dev...*" As Guruji starts quoting Sanskrit in the middle of his talk, he seems to become almost euphoric, as if he is riding on a wave of bliss.

"Let me have that fun in life, the knowledge that I gain in my life, let it always enter me. Hmm? With this simple thing, *Upanishad*, the student comes and 'sits near.' Sits near to learn more about his whole life and the mystery of this whole creation. Hmm?

"This is the biggest question in the mind, no? 'What is life?' 'Why am I here?' 'What is happening to me?' 'What is this world?' 'What is love?' 'What is knowledge?' All these inquiries. It's very fortunate that these inquiries come up in our mind.

"And then it needs to be understood. It cannot be read in the books, but lived, lived through. So one sits and undergoes the transformation. That is health, when we are transformed and the bud becomes the totally blossomed flower."

Gurudev's closing remarks recapitulate some of the topics (life, love, health, etc.) requested by the audience at the beginning of his talk. I feel humbled by the implied compliment to the newcomers who suggested them. Through that final story about Buddha, it seems to me that the master has, in a public address, led us into subtler depths of wisdom than at any previous moment of our silent inward voyage.

During the closing chants of the evening, I begin to feel strangely exhilarated, as if I myself may have just "sat and undergone a transformation" of some sort. What a crazy day this has been, rollicking back and forth from the ridiculous to the sublime, over and over and over again! Guruji's mischievous practical joke, and the multi-faceted wisdom it conveys, the raunchy letter about sex and the richly compassionate answer it inspires, the absurd tale of two kings and the deep understandings of Buddha that it leads to…My dizzy mind feels like it is climbing down from a careening carnival ride at a spiritual 4-H Fair.

After satsang, I wander back to the old cracked swimming pool. Other people on our course scarcely seem to notice this relic, but I pay my respects to it nearly every day during meditative walks, and have taken a fancy to its starkly arid charm. This evening, it beckons as one of my favorite solitary haunts. Even at midday, there is some shade down in the corners of the diving end, now deepened by moon-light into pools of mysterious gloom. My eyes adjust to the shadowy darkness as I creep down sloping slabs of cement into the most shrouded corner, from where like a frog in a midnight pond, I might contemplate the stars, seeing without myself being seen.

Sitting on the bottom here is probably ill-advised: there might be scorpions. So I make myself comfortable on my feet by leaning back with my shoulders against a crumbly section of the intersecting walls. Gazing from my softly triangular puddle of obscurity into the vastness of a twinkling, shimmering, blue-black sky, I leave the practical flotsam and jetsam of life to float away on its own, and sink into reverie.

How fathomless the mind of a sage! Beginning from my days as a youthful scholar, I fancy myself the uncompromising free spirit, acknowledging no obligation to intellectual hegemony in any form. And yet this day is confronting me with a living example of such untrammeled and free-ranging intelligence as puts my libertine mind to shame. No social taboo, no group expectations, indeed no boundaries of any sort ever seem to stand in Gurudev's way. On the basis of what I have witnessed this day, I suspect that absolutely anything might be employed, at any time, in the unceasing flow of wisdom and Grace he so simply yet mysteriously embodies.

If there is a key to this magnificent, boundless freedom, it certainly cannot be equated to my own intellectual habit of regarding nothing as sacred. On the contrary, what I find myself contemplating here is the freedom of an intelligence before whom there appears to be nothing that is *not* sacred...

This thought stirs up a wellspring of insight. I suddenly perceive that some of my most conscientious habits of mind are actually limiting and constricting the very intellectual freedom they intend to preserve! By regarding nothing as sacred, my mind in effect banishes the entire realm of the sacred from her legitimate domain of inquiry. I can see that this habitual stance is perpetuating a kind of stand-off between my mind and my heart: My heart's eternal yearning toward the pleasures of sacred communion have become an object of chronic suspicion to my freedom-thirsty mind. And this internal conflict has been externalized for decades in my deeply reserved demeanor toward my family religion, generating undercurrents of tension and estrangement between myself and my religious relatives—Mom and Dad in particular.

By swinging so blithely from mischievous to masterful, raucous to reverent, foolish to profound, Gurudev seems to be modeling an alternative premise for intellectual freedom and integrity by which some of my most intransigent conflicts and constrictions might be logically resolved. Regarding everything as sacred would banish nothing from the domain of inquiry, restore my heartfelt yearnings to intellectual legitimacy, and eliminate at least one major source of ongoing internal tension. I can't venture to predict how such an interior repositioning might ultimately affect my external relationships with family and religion, but I think these might become interesting areas of my life to watch…

Rousing myself from my musings, I begin to ascend from the pool. If indeed there is nothing that is not sacred, then why should I hesitate any further about appealing to Guruji for advice and assistance in dealing with sexual challenges? I surely owe it to my husband to leave no stone unturned that might help me overcome my marital shortcomings.

Ananda Mouse

Creeping back into my room, I quietly rearrange my blankets into a kind of tent over my head so I can write by flashlight without disturbing anyone. My pen pours out a saga extending to four pages of intensely personal prose, and opening with a note of permission to Guruji for discussing it before the group according to his discretion. If anyway everything is sacred, then it seems only fair to offer to share my story with those whose courageous openness has benefited me. Well after midnight, I finally snuggle into my pillow, feeling at peace and at one with the inner and the outer of it all.

Although we continue to observe silence, our morning meditations are now abbreviated to allow for a gradual rise of body metabolism toward the level required for ordinary activity. This clears time for a morning question and answer session with Guruji. My fat note perches conspicuously in the basket. I wonder anxiously what Guruji might do with it. In broad daylight, my calm and courageous resolve of the night is wimping out into quivering self-consciousness.

Expectant silence prevails for several minutes as Gurudev sorts through the notes, arranging them into little piles on his lap. Even though I am sitting two thirds of the way toward the back of the room, I can see clearly when he picks up and opens my note because it is so voluminous. My heart leaps into my throat as he studies its opening lines for several seconds and then consigns it to one of his piles.

Guruji opens the discussion by handing a couple of the shorter notes to the reader, but in my self-conscious state I am unable to focus on either of them. I do observe, however, that during the reading of the second note, he again picks up mine and starts looking at it. This does not appear to interfere with his ability to understand and answer the one being read, but it is very distracting to me. He repeats this subtle torture during both of the next two notes that he hands to the reader. This is driving me nuts! Is he deliberately pushing my quavering intensity to its uttermost limit, or what?

I close my eyes and take recourse to transcendence to calm my palpitating heart. This settles my nerves somewhat and shifts my angle on the issue at hand. 'Okay,' I think. 'Let me at least know where I myself stand. Do I or do I not want him to have this note read aloud?' As I fathom my own depths, I realize that in my heart of hearts I still feel as calm and sure and open as while writing in the night. It is just this surface part of me that is getting all worked up. Whether Gurudev chooses to have my note read or not, his choice will be from wisdom. I can leave it up to him.

Opening my eyes, I see that Guruji again has my note in his hand. Suddenly it occurs to me that in picking it up and looking at it, his intention is not to torture me, but simply to tune in on me, to pick up whether I from my side still feel okay with my offer to allow him to discuss it before the group if he wants to. As this thought passes through my mind, he hands my note to the reader:

"Dearest Gurudev,

"It is such a relief to have a master from our lineage who is open to discussing matters pertaining to sex..." Of course, the subject of sex again draws up laughter from the group, including the reader, who throws in a comment about "four pages" before continuing:

"I have been intending to make the following appeal in a private letter; but since the material touches upon many points which came up in the past few days' discussions, I have decided to give you the option of discussing it before the group, if you wish.

"My husband and I were married in 1979; and about two or three years later we had spontaneously developed a nearly celibate marriage, just exactly as you described. We were wondering about this; but as we had both made the conscientiously misguided choice to regard our guru as a 'world master,' who should not be bothered by personal questions, we never even considered asking him our question.

"Instead, when he sponsored an Ayurvedic tour that came to our city, we put this question to the *vaidya* (Ayurvedic physician)—an elderly Indian gentleman with very traditional ideas about the many childless American couples he was seeing. He advised us that absolute celibacy was not good for householders, and suggested that twice a week was not too much. We weren't even getting around to it twice a year!

This evokes more laughter, but the reader forges ahead: "So we decided to work toward a goal..." Here the reader has to pause for an eruption of raucous hilarity which completely drowns out his voice. As it subsides, he continues: "...of about once a month. It seemed like a healthy compromise. We had to work very hard to accomplish this." More laughter threatens to take over, which the reader successfully ignores. "The desires just weren't there. But gradually I discovered that at a particular point in my monthly cycle I could pick up a sexual flow, and in about two years we began to get back into what we believed was a more healthy sexual routine.

"A few years later, in the course of nature, I became pregnant, and immediately encountered a major health crisis. Some fibroid tumors I did not know I had, started growing rapidly and caused a miscarriage at three months, along with more serious infections, etc., which resulted in a six-week hospitalization. A surgery was necessary which resulted in a deep incision straight down my torso right through my navel.

"During recovery I became aware that my customary experiences of peace and bliss in meditation were drastically compromised, and in their place I was experiencing an unbelievable amount of sexual energy consistently and predominantly in the lower half of my body. My doctors saw nothing wrong with this, and advised me that I could enjoy as much sex as I liked; but I knew that this was not the life I wanted for myself. So I sought help from an alternative care provider, and found some excellent chiropractors and bodyworkers who were able to accomplish a lot of major re-wiring so that my energies do now once again circulate in fairly normal currents throughout my body. I also did two and a half years of extended meditation, which has restored my meditation experiences to a reasonably acceptable level.

"But there remains a chronic problem with me. I still sometimes experience sudden and intense sexual attractions to men. This mostly happens with my husband, which is no problem as he is very attentive to my needs even though he himself feels drawn, at age fifty, to more celibacy again. But it also occurs on some occasions with other men. I do not indulge this, but it is a chronic problem, which doesn't seem to be going away.

"Right now there are two men that I feel these feelings toward, in addition to my husband. Both of them are important colleagues of my professional life; and what I really want with them is warm, friendly, mutually respectful professional relationships, not torrid love affairs. But my system goes haywire sexually, sometimes when I even think of them. Both of them operate their sexual lives on rather different premises than I do, and each has on occasion become quite..."

When the reader stops here due to difficulty in reading the next word, the hushed silence, which has gradually overtaken the room, becomes almost as deafening as the earlier raucous laughter. Some of my course mates may be simply aghast that anyone would actually expose such intimate material to semi-strangers. But my deeper sense is that many are responding with respectful and heartfelt empathy to the unfolding of my tale.

Ultimately, the reader gives up with an apology, and reads on, skipping the illegible word: "quite...(I'm sorry)...with me over the sexual issue, seeing me according to the prevailing climate of opinion as being into heavy denial of my own sexual reality.

"I just don't feel that my husband, who is my best friend in the world and who is quite compassionately tuned in to what I am going through, deserves an unfaithful wife. I feel that these attractions to other men draw energy away from him and, at subtle levels, are actually aggravating an intense financial crisis he is currently dealing with. I also wish I could support him in his natural inclinations toward celibacy by joining him in going in that direction myself, but I am currently very far from that goal.

"According to my upbringing, attractions outside of marriage are called lust; and I am wishing that I could just ask you to take this away from me. If it is not quite that simple in my case, just please do what you can to complete the healing on all levels. Maybe I have some things I have to work through in all this, but could I just surrender it all to you, as it is, anyway?

"Thank you again for your willingness to attend to such a matter."

The sound of the reader's voice fades away; and Gurudev allows the silence to fill the room again for some time. Then he quietly and sensitively speaks:

"Hmm? When such a problem arises in you, raise the level of prana in you. Do more pranayama [breathing practices]. Do your ten minutes Kriya. You will see immediately that the energy which is flowing into the lower parts, will start moving upward. You'll feel that pull has reduced, and you'll feel more comfortable and easy."

Being given such specific personal advice about applying the practices really feels like quite an honor, especially the instruction, *"when such a problem arises...do your ten minutes Kriya."* This powerfully centering practice is ordinarily limited to once per day. I also find it marvelously uplifting to be given the tools for solving my problem autonomously. It seems to convey that the master has faith in me, and in my personal level of strength. At the end of his answer, I gesture namaste and bow my head toward the ground right where I am sitting. It is as if there is no one else in the universe except for him and me.

Toward the end of the morning, we begin the gradual process of coming out of silence. It is announced that in order to maximize Guruji's time with the group as a whole, we are being organized into small groups to meet with him semi-privately, instead of individually. Our small group audiences are to occur over an extended lunch break, after which the entire course is to re-convene, slightly later than usual, for the afternoon meeting.

My group falls third or fourth down the line, so I eat lunch while awaiting our turn. The first two groups meet outside under a tree, almost within earshot of the outdoor dining tables. However, since this has a tendency to attract onlookers from other groups, the rest of the meetings are re-located to one of the waiting rooms in Gurudev's personal suite.

Eventually the organizers call my group to assemble in the hallway outside the same door where I so nervously stood, at the invitation of my teasing friend, on the day of my arrival. This gives me occasion to observe, to my growing frustration, that my nervousness at the prospect of personal interaction with Guruji has not even slightly diminished since that time. If anything, it is even more intense. I sit on the floor and close my eyes, attempting to apply the instruction about observing the sensations; but my fight-or-flight anxiety is doing its usual number on me: My fearful emotions, instead of producing sensations in the heart like they are theoretically supposed to, are making themselves felt mostly in my churning gut; and being aware of them does not noticeably lessen my discomfort.

Very shortly the door opens, as smiling and laughing members of the previous group file out. While my group slowly files in, I notice that my teasing friend is serving as general monitor in the corner of the room. Guruji sits on a low couch along one wall, conferring with a straggler from the exiting group as we arrange ourselves on the floor in three semi-circular rows at his feet. I end up in the second row almost directly in front of him.

As soon as we are settled, Guruji greets us cordially as a group, and then begins to address various individuals at random. He seems to be reaching out to those who are fairly new or who have perhaps not expressed themselves much during the course. He then begins to look at each of us in turn, from one side of the room to the other, inviting us to speak if we wish. The woman next to me simply gazes into his eyes for an extended moment, before bowing namaste. I watch her with envy, wondering from where in the universe one might summon such awesome self-possession.

As he turns his attention to me, I turn my head in confusion and look over my shoulder, self-consciously concerned that he might be actually nodding to someone behind me. To clarify his intention, he speaks my name and inquires how I am doing. Overcome by inexplicable embarrassment, I mumble something politely affirmative. Inwardly I am furious with myself for so inanely wasting this priceless opportunity, but not even anger can prevail against the mysterious paralysis that overtakes me in the moment of face-to-face encounter with my beloved and revered Gurudev.

I continue to stew in my self-absorbed turmoil of frustration and self-castigation as Guruji attends to the others in the group—until the very last person, a shy and unassertive older gentleman, brings up a point which claims my attention. It seems that he, too, "like that woman who wrote that long letter," has been experiencing inordinate sexual desires in the aftermath of an abdominal surgery, in his case for cancer of the colon. He wants to know if he might follow the same instruction of raising the level of prana in his system by doing more pranayama and Kriya. Guruji responds in the affirmative. A wave of gratification wells up in my heart upon receiving such tangible evidence that the sharing of my story has been useful to someone else.

By some indecipherable logic, witnessing this exchange unravels my paralysis and mobilizes my tongue. Rashly oblivious to the fact that I am exposing the identity of "the woman who wrote that long letter" to about seventeen other people, I raise my hand and blurt out to Guruji that there is still one major concern I did not mention in my letter. He nods and listens as I explain that I actually still have a lot of fibroid tumors, which could not be removed without also removing my uterus. I give vent to my dread of the possibility of having eventually to face yet another surgery, and implore him to help me finish healing without that, if at all possible.

An odd look crosses Gurudev's face. He appears to turn inward for an instant, and then briefly responds with just the words, "We'll see." My heart skips a beat. Is he irritated with me? Have I been too bold in speaking out of turn? I continue to watch him closely, but he isn't giving me any further clues as he jovially dismisses our group.

I wander back to the empty meeting hall and sit alone in my cozy little cocoon of cushions and backjack, trying to understand the turmoil of emotion that chronically overtakes me in moments of relating to Guruji. It isn't like he is any kind of stern or formidable personage. On the contrary, he is so carefree and friendly and easy-going that most people find themselves talking and laughing and joking with him as comfortably as if they have known him all their lives.

So what is the matter with me? What makes me act so dopey in his presence? Why can't I even offer him a sensible, friendly conversation with my normal, intelligent, generally competent self? Where does all my habitual self-possession disappear to, and why, upon confronting my beloved Gurudev? As my mind fails to produce anything helpful on any of these points, it occurs to me that even this question might perhaps be put to Guruji. What the heck, I have written to him about everything else! I fish out my stash of paper from the pocket inside my backjack and contribute one last note to the basket.

On my way out of the hall, I encounter my teasing friend, who is scanning the grounds for stray members of the final group to meet with Gurudev. I take the opportunity to ask him if he may have been observing Guruji during his answer to my last minute appeal. He tells me he was in fact watching closely, and also saw that strange expression cross Guruji's face. But he has no more idea than I do what to make of it. Evidently, on this point, the intentions of the master are just going to remain a mystery. Anyway, I feel satisfied that I have now confided the entire matter of my health concerns into Gurudev's hands. Also, the more I think about it, his words *"we'll see,"* do seem to convey a promise of staying with me throughout my healing, what-ever direction it might take.

Most of my course mates are gathered in small groups about the grounds, exploring the pleasures of conversation after nearly a week of abstinence. As I begin to circulate, an old friend walks up to me and inquires if I am planning to drive through his city in Texas on my way home. I reply that I am, and does he need a ride? No, but he wants to invite me to stop and visit him and his wife and daughter, even stay overnight if I have time. He reminds me that I have yet to meet his daughter, a bright and affectionate eight-year-old who still cherishes the crib quilt I made for her before she was born. I thank him warmly and tell him that I have already made overnight arrangements, but promise to at least stop by for a visit while I am there. We reminisce together for several minutes. He and his wife had just succeeded in becoming pregnant shortly before my husband and I moved away from their city. Has it really been eight years since then? He gives me his address and phone number, and I give him a big hug. It will be a real pleasure to meet their little girl!

Expecting that Guruji would soon finish with the last small group, most of us start moving toward the hall, whose windows and rafters, attuned to the softness of silence and chanting and Gurudev's melodious voice, now have to adjust to the unfamiliar echoes of jovial conversation. As I make a detour to the water table in the back of the room, I overhear a few phrases from a soulful conversation about relating to the master. Intrigued, I approach and make eye contact with someone in the circle, who welcomes me by silently patting her hand on an empty cushion by her side. I smilingly accept the invitation, and sit down among familiar faces with unfamiliar names. A young Indian man at that moment responds to someone else's point: "In my country, there is a saying, 'Get naked before the guru.'" Other members of the circle greet this contribution with enthusiasm, while my own thoughts drift inward. 'Get naked before the guru.' The phrase seems hauntingly pertinent to something in my experience...

Before I have time to ruminate further, the guru himself walks into the hall, followed by a train of laughing and smiling course members. I stand up and return to my seat as Guruji ascends to the stage. As he sits down, we all follow suit. He reaches out for the Question Basket and fumbles though its contents. "Still a lot of questions in the basket. But you are all out of silence...What would we like to do now? Answer the questions? Hmm?"

The consensus of the group seems to favor this idea; and perhaps also he feels it would be best for us to break silence gradually by shifting back into listening mode for awhile. He begins to sort through the notes, and hands a few to the reader.

I notice that most of the notes selected for reading today are colored by the tender feelings that flow inevitably as dear friends approach the parting of ways. Quite a few contributions contain heartfelt expressions of love and gratitude and proffer no questions at all. To these Guruji responds with silent smiles or softly intoned affirmations: "Hmm," "Very good," etc. Lulled by the sweetness of these exchanges my mind drifts off into reverie. How quickly this week has passed, and yet how long ago and far away it seems since I was packing my bags to come...

Suddenly my mind is recalled into the room by the jarring cadence of a note that seems startlingly out of synch with the prevailing sentiments of the afternoon:

"I realize that it is not at all obvious from the way I relate to you, but I actually am an intelligent, competent person with a lot to offer on many levels. I would dearly love to make my best qualities more freely available to you, but for some reason every time I come into your presence or relate to you in person, I turn into such a dithering idiot..."

In horror, I realize that the jarring cadence is coming from *my* note, which is currently being read, with feeling, by a young female reader, who, to make matters worse, has just stumbled awkwardly over the word "dithering," repeating it two or three times, with different inflections, before she is satisfied she has got it right. By now I am convinced that the readers must be instructed to enter into the spirit of the notes they are reading; and usually I feel gratefully appreciative of their efforts. But at this moment I feel so humiliated, I can't even listen to the rest of my own words. Why couldn't my final note to Gurudev have contained some poetic expression of heartfelt gratitude instead of this crudely boastful and pathetically self-denigrating tirade of complaint and irritability? I sit like a stone, not daring to move a muscle lest I betray my own shame, for this is truly the one note I do not want anyone to guess the authorship of.

The silence that prevails after the reader's voice has subsided, seems interminable. No doubt she is waiting for some signal from Gurudev as to whether he is going to respond to my inquiry or have her read the next one. I chance a surreptitious glance at Gurudev's face, and see that his eyes are closed and his features completely immobile. Apparently he has sunk into deep samadhi. After one more endless moment, he opens his eyes and extends another handful of notes to the reader.

During Sri Sri's retreats, I often overhear expressions of frustration about his seeming capriciousness in answering some questions and not answering others; but this is the first time he has responded with silence to one of mine. I can't exactly say I am disappointed. In fact, I rather hope that he may have been so deep in samadhi as not to have heard it at all. If I could, I think I would choose to erase the past few minutes of my life from the akashic record altogether.

Gradually, my inner turbulence settles down, and I notice that there are more questions in the notes that are now being read:

"Dear Guruji,

"Why are there so many dysfunctional families, divorces and broken relationships today? Is the institution of marriage changing?"

Sri Sri: "Relationships are not supplemented by a relationship to the Divine. That is why this has happened. More acceptance is necessary, more understanding—more Art of Living programs—will all help to bridge the gap between people.

"See, when we fail to see a person as part of the Divine, or just a rag doll, stuffed doll, then we see them as personalities. Everybody is in a personality cult, other than the enlightened. Because everybody sees persons, persons, persons, persons. And seeing them as persons, then there are love/hate relationships one has. One doesn't see anyone as oneself. This is the basis of problem.

"If we start seeing everybody as rag dolls, just like the bubbles in the water, then you are in the *Brahman* [the unbounded absolute], you see the Divine. This type of understanding, when it arises with everybody in a family, then family remains more united. Before that, difficult." He nods to the reader to proceed with the next question:

"My holy master! What is the quickest way to smash the ego and dissolve? In all gratitude and love."

Sri Sri: "Quickest way is to see that it is not there. What you think is ego? Some pain, something, some embarrassment, some shyness, some pain—this is what is sign of ego, right? Just laugh at it. Laugh and let go. Just laugh at it, smile, and it's gone. Observe the sensations, it's gone. Be in devotion, in love, it's gone. And do the Kriya, it's gone. Be natural, it's gone. Be hollow and empty, it's gone.

"First of all you think you have a big ego, and then you are trying to chase it out. This is the trouble. I tell you, you have no ego. What is your ego? What are you? You're so insignificant. You are nothing. In this whole universe, you are nothing! From the plane you can't even look at you walking on the street.

"Just understanding. Be natural. Lack of naturalness is ego. Because one is used to it, you may feel—but know it's already dissolving, it's going, it's going, it's gone."

Certain phrases of this answer resonate poignantly in my mind: "...Some embarrassment, some shyness, some pain

—this is what is sign of ego, right?" He could be describing my own still throbbing experiences of trying to relate to him—the agonizing self-consciousness I feel while sitting in front of him in the small group, and my private sense of humiliation during the reading of my last note. How uncanny that he should choose the examples of shyness, embarrassment, and pain to illustrate "what is sign of ego"! From my familiarity with his discourses on the subject, I know that there are other angles from which he might approach this question. I get the strangest feeling that even now, two or three questions later, he may be attending to the appeal I made in my embarrassing note.

I cannot resist exploring in this direction. To what extent do his last few responses actually seem to apply to my "unanswered" question? In fact, there is something in his response to the inquiry about divorces and broken relationships, that also strikes a chord:

"Everybody is in a personality cult, other than the enlightened. Because everybody sees persons, persons, persons, persons. And seeing them as persons, then there are love/hate relationships one has. One doesn't see anyone as oneself. This is the basis of problem."

A flash of insight opens up a chain of connections in my mind: Of course! I have been seeing and presenting myself to Gurudev as a person, as if he is a person and I am a person, not as if he and I are both "oneself." In fact, I have been relating to myself as a "person," too, going through a "love/hate relationship" with myself, not even honoring *myself* as being one with myself. Under the spell of "personhood," I just now, during the reading of my last note to Gurudev, have been wanting to disown my very self in the midst of an intense and vulnerable moment! And that is because, functioning as a "person," I become so awkwardly conflicted that I manage to come across as both arrogant and self-deprecating, in the space of two sentences!

What a bizarre self-entanglement! Guruji is right: The shyness and embarrassment and pain that so baffle me are no doubt signs of my illusory ego, and the only sensible thing to do is *"just laugh at it. Laugh and let go."* I remind myself of a pet kitten, crying for help after getting foolishly tangled up in playing with a spool of thread, and then just having to sit still and purr while her human cuts her loose.

But Guruji himself is not laughing at me. My mind flashes back to that stolen glimpse of his deep inward stillness as my question is being read out, then flashes back further to a scene from my childhood:

One summer day while wandering through the woods on my father's farm, I spy a water snake lying in the sun on the opposite bank of the creek from where I am standing. Looking at it intently, I soon realize that it is amidst the throes of shedding its skin. For upwards of an hour, I stand transfixed as its wetly glistening new spots inch their way out of their still moist encasement of partly split scales. I scarcely dare even to breathe for fear I might scare the vulnerable creature into hurting itself by moving too quickly in its tender new hide. Eventually, the angle of the shadows warns me that the afternoon is waning; and I quietly steal away, concerned that someone from my family might come looking for me—and might not feel to honor the sacred rebirth that I feel so privileged to be witnessing…

Suddenly I realize that during the reading of my embarrassing note, Gurudev not only hears every word, but is also fully aware of the intensity of my inner experience—is in fact observing with fully empathic reverence as I pass through these painfully vulnerable moments in my own unfoldment,—no doubt perceiving layers of my truth that I myself can only vaguely discern. I can no longer doubt that he is quite intentionally responding to my awkward appeal through the exquisitely sensitive modulations of his answers to seemingly unrelated subsequent inquiries, and from a motive not dissimilar to my youthful concern to honor and protect the vulnerability of the aquatic reptile whose early summer molting I have been privileged to observe.

The day after my adventure with the water snake, I return to the same spot by the creek. The snake is gone, but its still damp, empty coil of scales is lying in the sand. I carefully pick it up for a keepsake, but have to discard it before I get even halfway home, because it smells really bad.

Pondering Guruji's indirect manner of responding to my final inquiry, I come to realize that for several days, like the snake by the stream, I have been going through the intensely vulnerable process of extricating myself from an outgrown "skin" of ego. But then as we re-emerge from our silence, I unconsciously attempt to retrieve my old familiar persona, only to discover that, like the smelly coil of snakeskin I attempt to take home from the creek, it is no longer suitable for me to keep at all…

Another image comes into my mind, of an analogy Guruji sometimes uses to describe the experience of death: He says that at the time of death, one looks down at one's body just like looking at one's discarded clothing on the bathroom floor. In a sense, I now find myself "looking down" at my decaying coil of discarded ego in a similar manner. Indeed, it would seem that my "inner game of Russian roulette" is actually presenting me with a kind of corpse,—an expiring persona through which my life and love simply can no longer shine.

So it is no wonder that I feel so self-conscious and vulnerable when confronting Gurudev! At every juncture where an ordinary friend might smooth over my awkwardness and bolster my ego by employing the usual social amenities—a few words of friendly ribbing, a jovial slap on the back, or whatever—Gurudev is responding from the silence of samadhi. He has been perceiving all along a deeper unfoldment, and reverently allowing it to run its course, undisturbed even by immediately relevant knowledge. Dedicated as he is to facilitating my growth and transformation, there is no way he is going to allow me any opportunity to lapse back into an outgrown condition. But then he also finds a way to administer the relief of wisdom and understanding as soon as its time is right. What could I possibly ever do to merit this much intimate care and attention from such a consummate master?

"In my country there is a saying, 'Get naked before the guru.'" Like a playful dolphin swimming up from the depths of the sea, the Indian gentleman's words resurface in my mind with a splash. Indeed, this would appear to be exactly what I have been doing! In fact, the word "naked" seems to offer almost a perfect metaphor for the agonies of self-consciousness with which I have been struggling since the very first day of this retreat. But I certainly did not come here with any such motivation in mind. I came here sailing free on a full mast of bliss and love. It almost seems as if I have been tricked somehow into this "naked" state…

I find myself musing over the spiritual dimensions of nakedness, whose imagery can be found in both Eastern and Western religious traditions. In the Biblical story of Genesis, Adam and Eve "discover" their nakedness (and get themselves expelled from the perfectly happy garden) after tasting the fruit of the Tree of the Knowledge of Good and Evil—a classic allegory for the universal human experience of falling from the blissful primordial unity of innocence into the dichotomy of egotism, where shame and conflict and suffering cannot be avoided. In the domain of ego, shame and painful self-consciousness are associated with nakedness, perhaps almost everywhere in the world.

According to the story of Genesis, it is the metaphorical serpent—the wily mouthpiece of ego—who tricks us into the embarrassing discovery of it.

But a spiritual passage through nakedness is sometimes associated with Divine reunion, as well. The Christian sacrament of Holy Baptism certainly contains a hint of this. In a famous story from the Puranas, the young teenage Krishna, with whom all the *gopis* [milkmaids] of his village are helplessly in love, mischievously steals their clothing as they are bathing in the Yamuna River. When they emerge from the water, they find that he has hidden their attire in the top of the tree where he is sitting, and they have to expose their nakedness to him in a gesture of supplication to get them back.

I can certainly identify with the poignant blend of ecstasy, agony, and hilarity that Krishna's gopis must have felt in that situation. Much the same blend of intense emotion characterizes my past few days with Guruji. In a sense, it could be said that while I have been bathing in the sacred waters, my Krishna has stolen my clothes!

Certain details of the saga of ego give me the feeling that a kind of whimsical poetic justice is ultimately ruling the universe. Like the emperor in the fairy tale, we get tricked into believing in the elaborate robes of self-imagery that we initially don in childish fantasy and play. Our invisible garb spun by our wily tailor gets sanctimoniously subscribed to by ourselves and all of our acquaintance—until some innocent savant blurts out the conspicuous truth which most of us are too befuddled even to see, much less say:

"But the emperor has no clothes!"

"I tell you, you have no ego!"

Perhaps because we are duped into believing it, we require to be counter-duped into seeing that it is not.

So what is the emperor to do, now that his nakedness stands unveiled?

"Be *natural*," Krishna smilingly replies.

Has the emperor any choice?

Sequel to Chapter Seven

A LITTLE SMILE INSIDE OF A BUBBLE

So as not to burn ourselves out after our week of rejuvenation in Santa Fe, my traveling companion and I arrange for a leisurely trip home. Our first overnight stay is with a girlfriend of mine who lives near and belongs to an ashram in Texas founded by another Indian spiritual master. The following day we accept her invitation to satsang and a meal there, which gives us an opportunity to experience a somewhat different flavor of the quest for enlightenment.

The white-haired "Swamiji" of this establishment speaks with an accent quite unlike Sri Sri's, rendering his discussions difficult for me to follow. My companion catches on quickly, though, and is able to engage him in answering some of her questions. He appears to emphasize the value of devotion almost exclusively. One of his major endeavors is to build a full-scale temple on the grounds, following ancient architectural principles detailed in Vedic scripture. The edifice is to be dedicated to Radha, Krishna's beloved gopi of Puranic lore.

Swamiji's ashram serves as a spiritual and cultural center for the Indian population of the area, sponsoring performances of music and dance as well as traditional religious ceremonies. Most of the actual ashram residents, however, are

Westerners, including several individuals I know from mutual association with other New Age interests. So I have no lack of friends and acquaintances to turn to for elucidation of unfamiliar customs and traditions.

One thing I ask about is the prefacing of their meal by sitting in reverent silence and watching as their Master eats his. This turns out to be a richly symbolic ritual, aimed at awakening the tender love of Krishna's gopi mother for her Divine Child in the hearts of the present-day devotees, as well as providing an almost tangible channel for the Master's Grace to flow to them via blessings conferred upon their food. I notice that many of the devotees subsequently eat their own meals in contemplative silence, - though not including the ones who are visiting with me, whose amusing anecdotes of ashram life assure me that ego dissolution is not being neglected among Swamiji's responsibilities toward his followers.

As I sit at the ashram dining table leisurely conversing with my friends, I inwardly perceive that since my retreat with Sri Sri, there seems to be a subtle lightness pervading every layer of my life. It is as if a little smile has been lit up inside of me, shining contentedly through all my actions, thoughts, and feelings, not ever becoming quite extinguished, even in sleep. Under the spell of this little smile, the most mundane details of my surroundings can delight me; and all my social interactions seem simple, charming, and fun,—though also somewhat inconsequential. Part of my light-heartedness appears to involve a droll disinclination to take anything or anyone very seriously, including myself.

Since my first encounter with Sri Sri, I recurrently find myself feeling as if I have walked into a fairy tale. Now, however, I am beginning to feel more like I may have walked into a cartoon. Guruji's fanciful description of higher consciousness pops into my mind: *"If we start seeing everybody as rag dolls, just like the bubbles in the water, then you are in the Brahman, you see the Divine."* It seems poetically suggestive of what I am experiencing. I often pass through seasons of dispassionate serenity during and immediately after extended meditation retreats, but there is something quaintly distinctive about this one. I wonder where it might be leading me.

As the evening progresses, one of my dining companions begins to embark upon a not very subtle campaign to convert me to his spiritual path. Inevitably, there will be missionary types in every group, blindly convinced that their particular spiritual Master, religious persuasion, political philosophy, marketing plan, therapeutic modality, brand of vitamins, or whatever, is *the* answer, and that anyone who does not subscribe to their exceptional Thing is more or less misguided. I am intimately familiar with this phenomenon, having been originally introduced to it by my mother, who has been modeling it for me since infancy with respect to her religion…

Even in adulthood, all of my siblings and I, with the possible exception of the one sister who is married to a clergyman, unanimously dread our mother's zealous attempts to return her wayward lambs to the sheepfold of the faithful. We dearly love her, and recognize, of course, that even though it drives us crazy, her obstinacy about religion is just part of her way of loving her children; for she really is direly concerned that we are all going to fry in hell if she doesn't somehow get us back into her church.

What we dread is not the fire and brimstone of our mother's dogmatic fears, but the way her adamant determination tends to create and enforce emotional barriers between herself and her children, semi-estrangements from which she and we mutually suffer. We know only too well how desperately she longs to have the kind of spiritually based communion with us that she enjoyed with her mother, full of tender mutual affirmations of the faith of our fathers.

But unfortunately, "faith," as understood by our mother and her church, means unquestioning adherence to beliefs and doctrines reflecting the patriarchal and authoritarian values and assumptions associated with several thousand years of volatile Middle Eastern history, the *Pax Romana*, and Medieval feudalism. In the course of living our lives, most of her children have found that we cannot, in good faith, continue to endorse many elements of that package; and we respect our mother (and ourselves) too much to simply lie to her. Tenaciously committed to the dogma of her church, she steadfastly declines to accept and appreciate the vibrant spiritual diversity which is flourishing in the healthy, successful, love-filled lives of her by now middle-aged offspring. According to her religion, God commands parents to guide their children, not follow them...

Anyway, my mother's strong-willed persistence probably deserves credit for a certain counter-strength in my own character: Inspired by her relentless dedication, I throughout my adult life steadfastly decline to subscribe to "only one right way" fundamentalism of any stripe. Usually when confronted with evangelistic overtures, I either change the subject or politely excuse myself.

This evening, however, my evangelistic friend gets quite a ways into his spiel before I notice that I have not yet experienced the shudder of revulsion which ordinarily warns me at the first hint of such a conversational turn. This isn't because I have any interest in abandoning my relationship with Guruji and establishing one with Swamiji instead. It is just that I find it so heartily entertaining to observe the character change in the friend who is sharing his zeal with me.

I know him from before as a lovable but distressingly self-centered playboy, somewhat taken with philosophy and esoterica, but really not going very much of anywhere with his life. The young man before me now, however, is centered, dedicated and committed, as well as clearly open to guidance from someone he recognizes to be wiser and more mature than himself. I cannot doubt that this represents several forward steps in personal growth for him.

To be sure he appears to be quite caught up in the illusion that the fountain of wisdom and Grace, which he has had the good fortune to discover, somehow represents the only reliable resource of ultimate truth on the planet. Nevertheless, his remarkable transformation inspires me to hope that he may be destined to blossom further, toward the mature depth and breadth of vision that his spiritual mentor is presumably modeling for him.

As I lie in bed in my girlfriend's guestroom at night, almost drifting off to sleep, my mind returns to the little smile inside of me. It is still there, quietly shining. Like a deep-sea diver revisiting the site of a recently discovered treasure, I spend a moment just being with it. Floating in its comforting glow, I pick up a dreamy sense that there is something it wants to share with me. Probing this mysterious intuition, my mind swims back a short distance in time, to the conversation with my evangelistic friend. How thoroughly I enjoy re-connecting with him, appreciating his new life, applauding his growth! It is thrilling to find him blossoming like this!

But something else, too: How amazing that I am relating to him with such warmth and openness even while he, in fact, drops several rather uncomplimentary and judgmental insinuations regarding my own Gurudev and the path my heart has chosen! I don't even feel the slightest bit uncomfortable with this! It is so astonishing, I almost have to wonder about the veracity of my perfectly clear and fresh recollection! I mean, this is a type of social intercourse I have dreaded and avoided all my life; and now all of a sudden I find myself participating in an instance of it, freely and uncritically, with open-hearted pleasure!

What, I wonder, could account for such un-me-like behavior?

"We are just a couple of bubbles," I think, recollecting Sri Sri's playful words:

"If we start seeing everybody as rag dolls, just like the bubbles in the water, then you are in the Brahman, you see the Divine."

Ha! Surprising as it is, I can see that in the midst of this conversation with my evangelizing friend, I am, in fact, so busy "seeing the Divine" in him – applauding his growth, enthusing over his potential – that I completely forget to get turned off or insulted by what he is saying and imply-ing with regard to me. His disregardful words and insinua-tions simply have no meaning for me. I only feel delight-ed, even honored, that he is sharing his heart so freely…

"Take every insult as a compliment," Guruji says, (illustrat-ing the point by that crazy tale about the two kings in India). *"Every insult can be taken as a compliment. Doesn't matter, you cannot be insulted, cannot be insulted at all. They are simply pouring out the stress or the tension or the anguish or the anxiety in them. So you receive it, take it. Hmm?"*

At the time while I am hearing Guruji speak these words in person, I seriously doubt whether my hot-tempered pitta nature could ever put them into practice. And yet I find myself this very evening living through them, almost to the letter, in a completely spontaneous way!

It would appear that my evangelistic friend is not the only one who has been going through changes lately. Ironically, in the very moment while I am marveling at the growth and transformation of my friend, similarly remarkable evidence of growth and transformation is coming out in my own behavior!

"What a dance," I think, feeling, like a bubble, somewhat tipsy and unanchored. "Bubbles meeting bubbles in the ocean, on our way to the top, where we pop, 'nobody' becoming 'everybody'..." My evangelizing friend, who has not lost his penchant for corny esoteric philosophy, would probably love this analogy,—if I could explain it to him.

My awareness floats back once more to that quiet little smile which continues to subtly illuminate my perception of inner and outer reality. It seems to suggest, with about the same friendly lack of gravity one would expect from a Disney World tour guide, that I might be witnessing a landmark personal event.

Truth cannot be told.

Words end where truth begins.

Words cannot capture existence, but silence can.

The purpose of words is to create silence.

—Sri Sri Ravi Shankar

The Inner Game of Russian Roulette 265

H. H. Sri Sri Ravi Shankar

About His Holiness,
Sri Sri Ravi Shankar:

He is born on May 13, 1956 into a prominent south Indian family with close ties to the late Mahatma Gandhi. As a young child, he is often found in deep meditation. At age four he surprises his parents by reciting the *Bhagavad Gita* (one of India's most revered ancient scriptures). He is fascinated by the rituals in churches, mosques, and temples, imitating them in play with his little sister. People notice that their chants and prayers always implore God to make everybody happy. He is a bit of a prankster, and has a mischievous tendency to give things away. He rebels against the practice, in his grandmother's village, of treating certain people as "untouchables," by intentionally hugging them, and then touching all his relatives' clothes and belongings before they can make him take a bath. At the age of eight, he begins to tell his playmates that he has friends waiting for him all over the world. In school, he declines to play soccer, because "these feet cannot kick anything." He is a magnetic, friendly, fun-loving personality, extremely popular with everyone.

Throughout his youth, he is fond of visiting saints and masters, who also take exceptional interest in him. Even in infancy, visiting saints offer *pranam* (a traditional form of bowing down in reverence) to him, and tell his parents that their child is the embodiment of a very great soul – or even, perhaps, "Divine." When he is fourteen years old, one of them tells his father, "I hear in your son's voice the sound of all the Four *Vedas*." (It is highly unusual for anyone to possess a natural affinity for more than one of the four most ancient, orally transmitted Vedic scriptures.) When someone brings him to see the renowned lady saint Ananda Mai Ma, she exclaims, "Ah, you have brought me the Ganges!"—indicating that he has a destiny to nurture, uplift, and purify the world. (The sacred river Ganges is considered to have a spiritually purifying influence upon all who bathe in it.)

His family provides educational opportunities appropriate

to their son's exceptional talents. They arrange for him to study Sanskrit with the venerable and exclusive Pundit Sudakar Chaturvedi (Sanskrit instructor and close associate of Mahatma Gandhi). His school teachers recognize his extraordinary intelligence, and accelerate his academic curriculum so much that by the age of seventeen he has acquired a Bachelor's degree in modern physics.

Under the guidance of the most qualified mentors, he devotes himself to mastering the practices and wisdom of the ancient Vedic tradition of knowledge. Barely past his teens, he is accorded the status and responsibility of being a Vedic *pundit* (scholar of the Vedic tradition), and begins to be called *Sri Sri,*—an expression of high regard which is difficult to translate into English. *Sri*, in general, conveys a sense of illustrious and radiant fullness. *Sri Sri* refers to "the two fullnesses"—i. e., the inner or *absolute* fullness of unbounded consciousness, along with the outer or *relative* fullness of brilliant thought, speech, and action.

At age twenty-four, Sri Sri emerges from a ten day period of *samadhi* (deep, silent meditation) to bring out the inspired rhythmic breathing practice of *Sudarshan Kriya*. It is a profound cognition which marks the beginning of his *dharma*, or life work. He becomes the founder of several non-profit educational and humanitarian organizations, emerging as a leading figure in human development and a multifaceted social activist. He travels to more than 40 countries a year to inspire leaders to balance business with ethics and social responsibility, to increase awareness and appreciation of how all the great spiritual traditions share common goals and values, and to offer personal guidance to his followers all over the world. His teachings of love, practical wisdom, and service promote harmony and encourage individuals to follow their chosen spiritual path, while honoring the paths of others.

Like Mahatma Gandhi (India's great Liberator and his family's beloved mentor), Sri Sri seeks to unite people of different traditions into a heart-felt communion based upon the universally cherished human values. In India, millions of Hindus revere him as one of their major religious and spiritual leaders, while people of other faiths look up to him for promoting inter-faith harmony.

About H. H. Sri Sri Ravi Shankar's work:

In 1981, Sri Sri founds the *VED VIGNAN MAHAVIDYA PEETH*, a free school for children from impoverished villages in south India. This initiative expands into the *CARE FOR CHILDREN* program, providing education and health care to thousands of disadvantaged children.

In 1982, Sri Sri begins teaching his *ART OF LIVING* Courses, designed to eliminate stress, create a sense of belonging, restore human values, and encourage people from all backgrounds, religions, and cultural traditions to come together in celebration and service.

In 1989, Sri Sri inaugurates the *ART OF LIVING FOUNDATION*, which is now active in over 140 countries, and, as a Non-Governmental Organization (NGO), works in special consultative status with the Economic and Social Council of the United Nations. In addition to an array of introductory and advanced self-development courses for the general adult population, the Art of Living Foundation offers numerous specialized programs for children, youth, the corporate sector, and people concerned with healing (both as practitioners and as recipients).

In 1997 Sri Sri founds a sister NGO, the *INTERNATIONAL ASSOCIATION FOR HUMAN VALUES* (IAHV) to advance human values in political, economic, and social spheres. IAHV is bringing sustainable growth programs to more than 30,000 rural villages in India, South Africa, and Latin America, and provides ongoing relief and reconstruction to areas affected by the tsunami, Hurricane Katrina, the Iraq war, and many other catastrophic events. IAHV's emphases include comprehensive rural development, education, tribal welfare, organic farming, micro financing, vocational training, trauma and disaster relief, conflict resolution, and rehabilitation programs for prisoners.

H. H. Sri Sri Ravi Shankar, with Ananda in her human form

About the author of the author:

Betty Ruth Krueger hails from a farm family in southern Indiana. She has an interdisciplinary Bachelor of Arts degree in sociology, psychology, and humanities from Valparaiso University. She lives with her husband of over thirty years in a Midwestern rural community, and serves as a volunteer meditation instructor in Sri Sri Ravi Shankar's Art of Living Foundation. Some of Betty's other interests include writing (her favorite obsession), singing in the choir at church, and Toastmasters (Betty and her husband participate as "outside members" of a Toastmasters club in a maximum security prison). Betty also enjoys gardening and working on the two-story Victorian home (a big old "fixer-upper") where she and her husband live and rent out guest rooms to supplement their retirement income.

Acknowledgements

All quotes from the Bible are taken from the King James Version.

All quotes by H. H. Sri Sri Ravi Shankar are used by permission of H. H. Sri Sri Ravi Shankar and the Art of Living Foundation.

Information about the Art of Living Foundation and its affiliates:

2401 15th St. NW
Washington, DC 20009

www.artofliving.org   Art of Living Foundation – USA

artdevivre.artofliving.org   North American Ashram, Quebec, Canada